VEGAN FOR FIT

VEGETARIAN AND CHOLESTEROL FREE FOR A NEW, HEALTHY BODY

FOOD PHOTOS Simon Vollmeyer • **FOOD STYLING** Johannes Schalk

QUANTITY CALCULATOR

We want to make your shopping trips easier. For each recipe, you can calculate the ingredients you will need for the number of people you are cooking for using the **Vegan for Fit Calculator** on the publisher's website **www.bjvvlinks.de/1005** You can then print the list out or pull it up on your smartphone.

VEGAN
FOR FIT

"In 30 days, you can lay the foundation for a healthy life and begin to make your dreams come true!"

ATTILA HILDMANN

DISCOVER A TOTALLY NEW HEALTHY BODY!

TABLE OF CONTENTS

8

LOSING WEIGHT
AND GETTING HEALTHY
begin in your head

We are all born into a system in which it seems normal that many of us are overweight or suffer from diet-related diseases. And it seems normal to us that we ourselves are a few pounds overweight—even if we don't feel comfortable in our own bodies.

For me, I finally got to the point where I no longer wanted to live in my overweight body. I asked myself what makes me different from the models in men's and fitness magazines. I also asked myself why I couldn't simply be fit and attractive—like so many other people. And every time I looked in the mirror, I got discouraged again because it seemed impossible to ever get rid of this unwanted layer of fat.

I had tried out almost every diet that was on the market at the time. Years passed, and I was still searching for the perfect nutrition system that would make me feel full and thin. The diets I tested were as difficult as they were useless. Each time, it was terrible; I gained the pounds back and they went right to my hips.

Up to now, my story sounds pretty hopeless. But really, success for each and every one of us only takes a small mental change: a simple agreement with yourself that from now on you simply do not question.

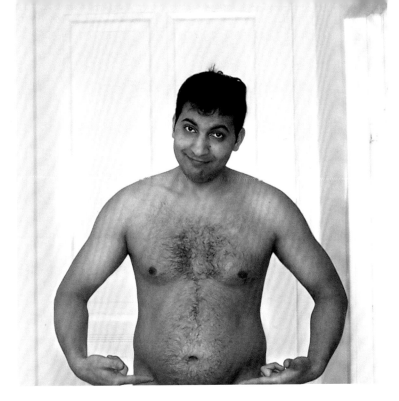

The years of being fat are over for me. I'm now enjoying life again and am very active. I've totally changed my eating habits. What no one can hardly believe is that I'm as much of a gourmand as I was before.

"It just took a very small step."

HOW TOUGH CAN IT BE?
30 days aren't that long!

Somewhere along the way, I began to understand that there is little in life that is free. You have to do something in order to have a healthy, beautiful body. And you have to have a way to get there that is doable.

Vegan for Fit is doable—and that makes it fundamentally different from many things out there that are called a diet. *Vegan for Fit* isn't a diet, but rather a very healthy way of eating; it's easy to follow, satisfying, and delicious. And it will help you to take off the pounds. At first, this might sound like a hoax, but the secret lies simply in a low-carb, plant-based diet. Although the scientific basis for this type of diet has long been known, it has never been implemented this consistently in a food plan. The two main reasons for this have been a lack of delicious recipes and the firmly entrenched belief that you cannot eat a "non-animal" based diet and still enjoy it.

Two of the most famous non-believers were Stefan Raab, who hosts the German late-night show *TV total*, and Steffen Hallaschka, who moderates the German television show *Stern TV*. They were both simply amazed how delicious and hearty a vegan dish can be. After the first samples, a gourmet chef on the show who had cooked a substantial meat dish had to admit defeat to the audience's preference for the healthy, low-calorie alternatives.

All the recipes were developed using the most advanced nutritional knowledge and weren't in any way influenced by the food industry—they have been proven in trials with test subjects and refined in the kitchen over a period of several months, so that even fast food junkies will be getting their money's worth and be able to stay with it.

So just forget about the frustration that you feel about not having yet reached your goals. Make up your mind, that beginning tomorrow, you will no longer accept any carelessness or laziness. Get up and do something for your well-being! Simply understand that it really is possible and this one small decision is guaranteed to lead you to success, when you cease to question it. Just this one sentence, this one decision will change your life forever: "I will do it for 30 days!"

In the accompanying booklet, you will find real stories of Challengers who thanks to *Vegan for Fit* developed a completely new feeling about their bodies and unexpected new food preferences.But more on that later! Think like a stonemason who is carving a statue made of stone, and at the beginning only has a vague idea what his or her sculpture will look like in the end. Lay the foundation for your dream body in your mind—the mind is your battlefield!

THE VEGETABLE TURBO
How your life will change in only a few days

A vegan diet is attractive for weight loss not only because it contains fiber-rich ingredients that make you feel more full and fruits and vegetables that have a higher density of nutrients, but also because it contains so-called phytonutrients, and other fat-burning elements. *Vegan for Fit* is the most nutrient-rich diet imaginable that will start the vegetable turbo in your body. In less than two days, you will begin to notice positive changes. You will feel lighter, energized, and satisfied and will easily lose those pounds of fat. If you look at the latest scientific studies, you can see that a lot of animal products are suspected to be linked to lifestyle diseases. In fact, it has been verified that too much red meat can lead to colon cancer. Milk, which is actually only meant for baby animals, can't be the ideal choice for adult humans. A large number of critical scientific studies confirm the disadvantages of drinking milk. Incidentally, no other species on the planet drinks the breast milk of another mammal.

I didn't become a vegan overnight, but the more I informed myself, the more I was convinced of the facts, and the more I changed my eating habits. Today, I insist on organic vegan ingredients. After I removed dairy products from my diet, for example, my acne and eczema disappeared within four weeks. It is the polyphenols, vitamins, and minerals that maintain our metabolism and protect us from environmental damage. Our body is constantly under attack by free radicals. These are atoms that simply tear the electrons off of the other atoms in our bodies, and thus damage cells. We begin to deteriorate at the level of our smallest components, that is—we begin to age. To prevent this as much as possible, it is important to eat a diet rich in antioxidative protective substances. In the world of science, the antioxidant potential of foods is known as the ORAC value, which is short for Oxygen Radical Absorbance Capacity. The higher the ORAC value of a food is, the more it is capable of protecting our bodies from harmful oxidative processes, thereby protecting against aging. In the laboratory, these harmful free radicals are chemically produced and then a sample antioxidant is added—such as some fruit or spices. This step neutralizes the free radicals and the ORAC value for the respective food can be calculated. Near the top of the list of foods with the highest ORAC value are vegan foods such as acai, cloves, ground vanilla, cocoa, herbs like thyme, oregano, and marjoram, and matcha green tea. Animal products are not on the list because they are not able to protect our body from free radicals. Rely on the facts—use a protective plant shield to guard yourself against negative environmental influences!

SUSPICION IS ADVISED.
Behind every diet, someone is earning money

When I was overweight, I really did try almost every diet on the planet—and none of them were able to help me keep my weight down in the long run. Although losing weight was always a goal for me, pure enjoyment is also important for me in my life, and if a diet didn't include this, there was no way that I would have been able to stick with it for very long.

What I find disturbing about many other "revolutionary diets" is that they contradict current scientific findings. And every day, new and ever more absurd diets are released on the market, and these were probably developed in a marketing department rather than as part of a nutritional study. When I ask around in the gym, I hear that many people are following a protein diet, where they eat primarily large amounts of animal protein and drink chemical protein shakes. How long will that work for them? If you take a look at the diet forums, you find many desperate people who are trying one system after another, and some even have their stomachs stapled because they don't see any other way to really feel full.

Although many diet systems often describe human beings as combustion engines, this is not what we are: we are living organisms which benefit from the many effects of polyphenols. Consuming only macronutrients—fats, carbohydrates, and protein—and supplementing with a few multivitamins cannot lead to a healthy and efficient body, even if you do lose weight.

I can remember that I went through a phase in which I only drank diet shakes. They were full of chemical sweeteners, and also contained a number of artificial flavorings. And they were expensive. I felt sick already after the first shake. In total, I was able to last one week. I lost weight, but my acne came back, and I felt bad emotionally. I was plagued by constant hunger pangs. In the end, I couldn't stand it any longer. I made myself a big plate of spaghetti and piled bacon on top. The next day, I had gained back half the weight that I had lost up until that point.

Diets are a billion dollar market. That is why new promises such as the following are constantly being advertised: "Your dream body in just 10 days." "More muscles in just one week." "Nine pounds in just 3 days." And recently there was also a diet where you had to decide if you were a hunter-gatherer or a farmer. According to this diet, both of these types have very different nutritional requirements, and if you're a farmer type, you're only too fat because you just don't understand the basics of nutrition.

Or someone invents a banal cabbage soup diet, which would be hard for me—a crash diet where you eat only cabbage soup, which is neither balanced nor very likely to bring success in the long run. Or even worse are diets named after academic figures—such as the Max Planck Diet, which causes everyone to immediately think of the Nobel Laureate Max Planck, who actually has nothing to do with the diet. In almost every case, it is the same system that is being used: a trick that supposedly allows you to outwit the laws of nutrition and energy balance.

IT WORKS A LOT BETTER WITHOUT ANY TRICKS

In fact, we don't need any tricks because when our fat reserves are high, our body is ready to release fat. It's enough to eat properly over a longer period of time and to burn off more calories than you consume. That's what our body is designed to do naturally, as long as we have fat reserves. And with the right diet, this method will work and you won't have any nagging hunger pains. The Challenge participants have reported a similar experience.

To experience success, you have to remember the basics: What types of food are really necessary? And what do our closest biological relatives who are never overweight eat? How can we use fruits, vegetables, salads, nuts, good oils, and legumes in a way that makes them delicious?

In the past eleven years—and especially during my 90-day Fitness Challenges that I began in 2011—I have developed a variety of delicious vegan dishes that meet all the nutritional requirements and still taste really good.

You should approach *Vegan for Fit* critically, but also listen to your own body. I am firmly convinced that you too will soon be impressed by the food and the accompanying effects of the Challenge.

WHY A SUCCESSFUL WEIGHT LOSS DIET SHOULDN'T BE A STARVATION DIET

It is important that your metabolism stays active. If you eat too little, your body goes into starvation mode, and as soon as you start eating more calories, it immediately stores them as fat deposits. Diets which require you to starve don't bring any long-term success.

What comes after the diet phase? We eat again, as we did before; in the best case, we continue to follow the basics of the plan—but sooner or later the pounds of fat are back on our hips because our body wants to return to its old shape. The body simply believes that the old reserves must have been necessary. Only about one to two years after reaching an ideal weight, does the body give up the desire to return to its earlier form—provided that in the meantime you have maintained your desired weight.

Long-term dedication paired with delicious enjoyment is the key to a lean, healthy body. Starvation diets are, in contrast, full of nutritional deficiencies, which might later cause health problems. Hunger pangs can also cause us to suffer emotionally and we are then often no longer in a position to work productively.

A fitting example is the many girls who are anorexic. Since they want to be thin like models, they eat very little. And the food that they do eat has so very little nutritional value that they lay the foundation for many diseases that manifest later in life, such as osteoporosis, which is caused by not consuming enough calcium. However, today, even supermodels are paying attention to their diet—many even eat a vegan diet!

With the *Vegan for Fit* recipes, you have a big advantage: you will feel full after eating amazing meals and you will satisfy your culinary needs. At the same time, you will lose weight because the foods are rich in fiber and contain lots of vital substances. This will keep your digestion on its toes and give your body just what it needs. Starving is out. Sustainable enjoyment is in.

THE CHALLENGE

A 30-DAY VACATION
for your body

BUILDING MUSCLE WITHOUT ANIMAL PRODUCTS?

It has long been proven that there is a close connection between animal products and diet-related diseases. For me, as an ambitious athlete with increased protein needs, that meant finding ways that I could feel good without animal products.

Today, I know that building muscle without meat is not only possible, but that it also has many benefits. The reason is simple: by eating a plant-based diet, I have a lot more drive and energy. In fact, this is something that most vegans experience strongly after only a very short period of time. Meat and animal fats make you feel full, but they also make you lethargic. The same applies to dairy products, which contain female hormones.

This may be connected to the fact that animal products are full of saturated fats, and that they don't contain any polyphenols and hardly any vital substances. They do however contain large amounts of cholesterol. And cholesterol is something which humans don't even need to consume. The body can produce the cholesterol it needs by itself and then excrete or deposit the surplus. Animal products also lack fiber, which after a few days of an unbalanced diet can lead to a virtual shutdown of digestion. Globally, doctors and scientists are now recommending that people move away from eating so many animal products—which is very controversial, as these products are a big factor in our economy. If you think this recommendation through, you can actually only decide to try to eat a diet that doesn't include any animal products.

There are many reasons why a plant-based diet can help you reach your goals during the Challenge more easily. To start with, plant products contain innumerable essential vitamins and minerals, and you will stay full and satisfied longer. And what is more, the human body can absorb the protein profile of plant products such as tofu, quinoa, and amaranth particularly well. It can do this because plant products all contain the essential amino acids (protein building blocks) in a balanced ratio. Recently, in Germany, an advertising slogan for a brand of extremely sugary yogurt for children claimed that it was "as nutritious as a small steak." The content of this claim is completely outdated. Finally, plant products are the only place you will find the fat burner molecules that help to speed up weight loss.

Vegan for Fit is balanced in all of its nutritional elements and is currently the diet that is richest in vital substances, and with which you can lose a significant amount of weight.

WHY 30 DAYS
without white flour

The Challenge recipes are free of white flour for one simple reason: white flour is nothing but empty calories. And it is made up of long-chain sugars, which although they supply our body with energy, they neither protect it with vitamins and minerals, nor ensure that key processes in our body continue to function.

And yet, unfortunately, we constantly eat flour products such as pasta, baguettes, bread, pizza, and cake. Whole-grain products are a good and healthy alternative. The important substances that our body needs are found in the shell of the grain, and this is largely absent in white flour.

Just look at the Stone Age people: they ate primarily roots, berries, fruits, grains, and occasionally meat when the hunt was successful. Naturally, white flour products were not part of their diet. The Challenge diet tries to align itself closely to the original needs of the body and therefore draws from this prehistoric diet. It is however supplemented by vegetable protein sources such as legumes, tofu, amaranth, and quinoa, which our body can optimally utilize.

Only later, when people settled down and the population exploded, did it become more common to plant various types of grains as a way to feed more people. In the time following, the first lifestyle diseases such as obesity began to appear. Incidentally, whole grains were scorned in the Middle Ages because they were not considered to be "pure" enough.

Let's take a look at what 100 g of spaghetti made with white flour contains in terms of calories, vitamins, and minerals, and then we'll compare this with pasta made from zucchini:

	100 g Spaghetti made from white flour	100 g Spaghetti made from zucchini
Calories	362	19
Carbohydrates	71 g	2.3 g
Vitamin A	0	50 µg
Vitamin B1	0	0.1 mg
Vitamin C	0	16 mg
Potassium	0	200 mg
Fiber	No	Yes
Polyphenols	No	Yes
Protein	12.5 g	1.6 g
Fat	1.2 g	0.3 g

We have a choice: simple carbs with substantially more calories in the form of pasta, which makes us tired and rundown or crispy zucchini noodles, which supply us with many essential nutrients and help make us firm and sexy. And we can even eat a lot more of them, in comparison almost 2 kg of zucchini—a huge pile of noodles! With a delicious sauce, the difference in flavor is much less than most people would expect.

We can, of course, eat starchy products now and then, but not after 7 o'clock and not too much. Whole grains are also allowed in moderation. Even better, though, are recipes that include quinoa and amaranth, which provide our body with all the essential amino acids we need and at the same time, contain a greater variety and a larger amount of those minerals than whole wheat.

So, let's think about it: crisp vegetables give us a lot of energy plus a refreshing kick, but they have a low energy density (calories). Whenever we can and whenever we feel like it, let's return to fresh alternatives!

For me, the purest form of luxury is unrestricted access to fresh foods that can give us physical and mental balance and lifelong health. I would rather have that than a fast car, a luxury villa, or dream vacations.

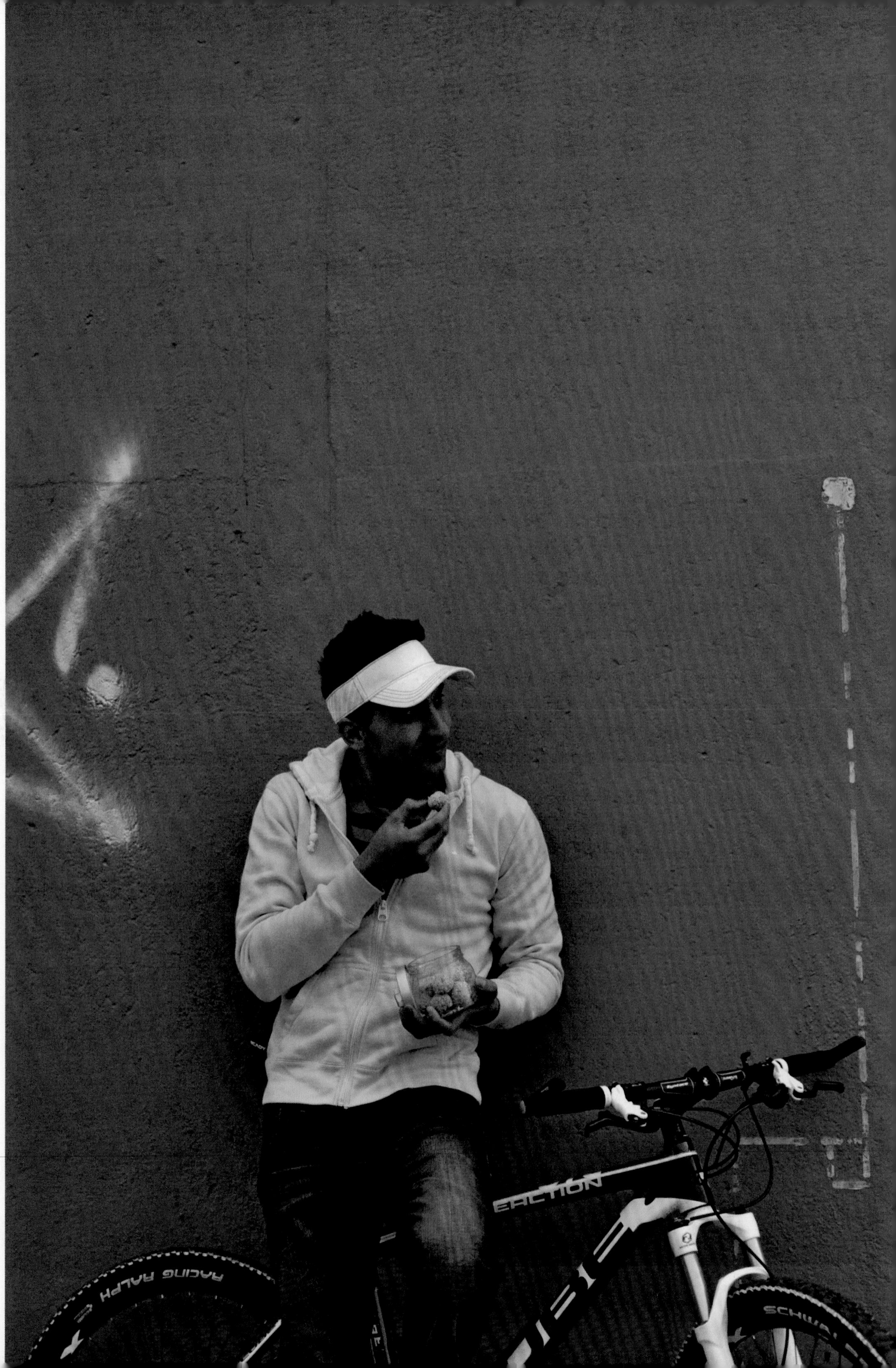
RACING RALPH

WHY DOING WITHOUT SUGAR IS NOT DOING WITHOUT

Industrial white sugar contains neither vitamins nor minerals and is merely a sweetening agent that doesn't have any kind of nutritional value and is often connected to diabetes and high blood pressure. In addition, it causes your blood sugar to go up rapidly and quickly sink again. The result: we get tired and hungry. Particularly when you are focusing on weight loss, this is not a good pattern because it leads to a higher intake of calories.

Furthermore, sugar can make your body more acidic and messes up the acidic-alkaline balance in your body. It has been scientifically proven that sugar causes cavities. Bacteria changes sugar into acids, which then corrode your teeth—and cavities appear. Sugar has also been repeatedly connected to the emergence of cancer.

Raw cane sugar does contain more minerals and is much more flavorful than white sugar; however, it has exactly the same effects and should therefore only be enjoyed in small amounts—and not at all during the Challenge! I prefer to choose natural sweeteners such as apple syrup, coconut palm sugar, dates, and most often agave syrup—all of these can be found in organic grocery stores and many supermarkets. Although stevia is also a possibility and doesn't have any calories, I have never particularly enjoyed the taste.

Organic agave syrup can be found most anywhere today, even in drug stores. Agave syrup is 1.4 times sweeter than sugar, dissolves easily in fluids, and has a pleasant taste. You should however also use this healthier sweetener sparingly. As for me, I'm not going to go so far as to drink my morning matcha shake unsweetened. It's simply a question of the right balance.

WHICH COMPLAINTS
can disappear in only 30 days

Here is an overview of the experiences that the first 100 Vegan for Fit Challengers had. When I read these points, the number of changes that took place here in such a short amount of time seems almost magical to me.

MANY OF THE CHALLENGERS REPORTED THE FOLLOWING:

- significant weight loss
- better digestion
- a surprising increase in strength and endurance
- a pleasant neutral body odor and taste in the mouth
- cleaner, firmer skin that looked younger and glossy hair
- increased ability to concentrate and more tranquility
- a better mood, up to euphoric feelings of happiness
- less need for sleep and increased sexual drive
- more desire to be active
- feeling of fullness without food cravings
- pain-free menstruation (female Challenger)

A FEW CHALLENGERS REPORTED THAT THE FOLLOWING IMPROVED (OR DISAPPEARED):

- eczema
- chronic inflammation caused by calcium deposits on the tendons
- mild cellulite
- bloating and constipation
- chronic fatigue and listlessness
- irritation of the digestive system (irritable bowel syndrome)
- blemishes
- snoring
- allergies

A few Challengers did report some small aches and pains: sore muscles from overexertion and bloating from eating soy products.

EVERYTHING YOUR BODY
will certainly not miss for 30 days

It's important that you know exactly what things you will not be eating for 30 days. You will find that the true secret to health really lies in leaving out chemicals, hormones, and preservatives, as well as anti-caking, separating, and coloring agents. The actual impact of all of the following substances is not known, which is one more reason to do without them and carefully watch which ailments disappear.

YOU SHOULD OMIT THE FOLLOWING:

- preservatives
- so-called natural flavoring agents
- anti-caking and separating agents
- stress hormones (residues in the meat of slaughtered animals)
- antibiotic additives (in many animal foods)
- residues from "gas flushing" of packages
- gelatin (from bones)
- sweeteners
- coloring agents of all kinds
- emulsifiers
- acidifying agents
- stabilizers
- hydrogenated fats (e.g., still in some margarines, frying oils, and pastries)
- flavor enhancers

If you are going to eat a vegan diet, you need to include Vitamin B12. This vitamin can then be stored in your body for over a year. You should also make sure you have a sufficient intake of Vitamin D and iron—however, this is also recommended for "normal" diets.

A large number of minor ailments often disappear all by themselves when you make sure to leave out the things listed above. And some problems disappear in an amazingly short amount of time. Many additives have immediate effects: hydrogenated fat and sugar (in cookies) can cause susceptible individuals to get heartburn within just a few minutes, and too much sugar can cause dandruff to appear after a few days and perhaps lead to cavities and toothaches over time.

Large quantities of meat can, for example, cause one to develop gout. Rheumatic patients are therefore often advised to incorporate a vegan and sugar-free phase into their diet each year in order to slow down inflammatory processes.

SOME CONCRETE EXAMPLES OF UNDESIRED CONSEQUENCES

For some time, artificial sweeteners have been suspected of causing cancer and other diseases.

The low, but constant supply of antibiotics coming from the daily consumption of meat from factory farms causes the pathogens in our body to become resistant. We then develop a resistance to important antibiotics. Multi-resistant germs develop and often result in many complications for older and weaker people.

Many processed foods and instant cake fillings contain gelatin—a product that comes from ground animal bones. In the days of the BSE scandal, bovine gelatin was particularly criticized because manufacturers couldn't prevent bone marrow remnants from the animals' spines from being ground in. And the bone marrow contained high quantities of BSE pathogens.

Flavoring agents often originate in a laboratory and are frequently made of unappetizing raw materials—such as sawdust for the strawberry flavor in yogurt. Up until a few years ago, human hair was used as the basis for obtaining cysteine, an amino acid used to make dough more elastic. At an organic grocery store, though, you will rarely come across these chemical additives that alter food to make it keep longer, to give it a fresh-looking color, or to be able to push it through production tubes without leaving any residue. The fact that bacteria and fungi don't appear on the sandwich spreads found in a conventional supermarket for weeks sounds desirable. But you should consider if every day you really want to be eating the things that prevent bacteria from growing.

For the next 30 days, simply take everything out of your shopping basket that you don't need and allow your system to reboot. Buy and cook fresh ingredients, and give your body energy without chemicals. When the 30 days are over, you will be amazed how reluctant you will be to return to a "normal" diet. Almost all of my long-term test subjects have reported a similar experience.

WHAT "SUPERFOODS"
Can Do For You

"Superfoods" are plant-based foods that contain lots of micronutrients. These include polyphenols, vitamins, and minerals. Animal products don't provide any polyphenols and are merely suppliers of macronutrients that contain a very small amount of vitamins and minerals.

Superfoods are said to be very beneficial and have anti-aging and protective properties. As often as we can, we should add these foods to what we eat as they provide us not only with the macro, but also with the necessary micronutrients. To do this, you don't have to completely change your diet. Just add a few goji berries to your smoothie or jam, mix some matcha green tea into your raspberry ice cream or shake, or use high-quality organic cocoa in the cake you're baking—it's really easy to increase the nutritional value of your normal meals. By reading current studies on nutrition and the prevention of lifestyle diseases such as cancer, it quickly becomes clear which foods have a protective effect. These include berries, cabbage vegetables, ginger, garlic, green tea, soy products, tomatoes, red grapes, onions, and spices such as oregano and turmeric. The healthy organic foods in the recipes found in this book combine together to have a very positive effect—here are some of the highlights.

AMARANTH

Amaranth was a sacred food among the Incas and Aztecs. The reason for this becomes apparent when you look at amaranth's nutritional value: 100 g of amaranth has twice as much calcium as 100 mL of milk and also a lot of iron, potassium, phosphorus, zinc, and the amino acid lysine. The Aztecs believed it had life-extending effects—no surprise for such a powerhouse food, which is now even popular with astronauts.

Warning: amaranth is available in both popped and unpopped versions. For the Firestarter Shake, the Amaranth Yogurt Pop, and the praline recipes, I use popped amaranth, and for the Zucchini With Amaranth Filling, I use the original unpopped version that you have to cook before eating. If you use the wrong type of amaranth, you will have a grinding experience with the pralines and instead of landing on the couch smiling with a praline in your hand, you might end up at the dentist office.

BERRIES

Berries are not only delicious, but also very healthy and rich in anti-cancer molecules such as ellagic acid, and proanthocyanidins and anthocyanidins. They also contain many vitamins, minerals, and polyphenols, and are even known for their skin-firming properties. For me, fresh berries with homemade almond milk or Strawberry Almond Kiss Ice Cream (For recipe, see p. 193) is a perfect start to the day. If we look into the past, we see that in addition to nuts, seeds, and occasionally meat, berries played a large part in the diet of our Stone Age ancestors. Our body is therefore perfectly suited to berries. Goji berries are rich in fiber and amino acids, and they contain lutein and zeaxanthin—substances which are good for the eyes, and are said to be capable of preventing macular degeneration, a degenerative disease of the eyes. Goji berries taste as if a raisin had had sex with black tea. Unfortunately, many berries come from areas that are so polluted with pesticides that they cannot qualify as organic. But you can choose aronia berries, which are native to the northeastern part of the United States, grown in Europe, and sold at organic grocery stores. Or you can use acai berries, which are rich in antioxidants and contain Vitamins B1, B2, B3, C, and E as well as phosphorus, calcium, potassium, Omega-3 and Omega-9 fatty acids, and the group of phytosterols. At organic grocery stores, you can also find delicious acai juice, which can be used, for example, to add nutritional value to your green tea. Acai fruit pulp is also delicious and is wonderful in an ice-cold smoothie.

GREEN TEA

Green tea contains, among many other substances, the molecule epigallocatechin gallate (EGCG), which is reputed to have a strong cancer-preventive effect. In addition to caffeine, a large amount of theobromine is found in green tea, which has an effect similar to caffeine, but lasts longer. This helps you to remain active all day. Green tea has a very high ORAC value; that's the value which measures the antioxidant potential. The king of green tea is matcha—a green tea which is shaded longer and finely ground. I drink it in my famous matcha shakes with oat milk. Matcha has an even higher ORAC value than normal green tea that is infused (Matcha types Fuku & Tsuki: 1700 ORAC units, Matcha type Hikari: 1573 ORAC units). It also contains the amino acid L-theanine, one that has both a stimulating and calming effect at the same time and increases the formation of alpha waves in the brain, which arise in the state of relaxation—such as during meditation. It therefore makes sense that matcha is the cult drink of Zen Buddhists and was the traditional drink of the samurai, the warrior class of ancient Japan! Generally, I drink only water, infused green tea, and matcha shakes. Nothing else comes in my glass (I don't like cups).

GARLIC

Garlic contains large amounts of alliin. When a clove of garlic is crushed, alliin comes together with the enzyme alliinase to create allicin, which works as an antibacterial agent and can protect against several kinds of cancer, including prostate and colon cancer. In addition, garlic just tastes great—both raw and after having been sautéed in oil.

CABBAGE VEGETABLES

Cabbage vegetables, including white, red, and green cabbage as well as cauliflower and brussel sprouts contain glucosinolates, which can trigger a whole chain of anti-cancer processes. Broccoli and other sprouts also contain many health-promoting substances and lots of protein. I really enjoy eating cabbage as cole slaw or as a tasty roulade with a savory filling. A true culinary highlight is seared red cabbage with a little saffron. Generally, you should only cook cabbage a short amount of time and chew it thoroughly, so that all of its protective agents remain intact and can be released.

TURMERIC

Turmeric is an important ingredient for curry. It is anti-inflammatory and has a long tradition within Ayurvedic medicine. Turmeric contains the compound curcumin, which is thought to have a cancer-preventive effect. This effect is potentiated by the compound piperine found in black pepper. I put a pinch of turmeric in almost every dish and in my shakes.

OMEGA-3 FATTY ACIDS

Hemp and flax oil contain particularly high levels of Omega-3 fatty acids, which act as anti-inflammatories. Often we don't eat enough Omega-3, but instead we end up eating too much Omega-6 fatty acids. (e.g., in sunflower oil). Canola oil also contains Omega-6 fatty acids. The term "Omega-n fatty acid" refers to the position of the first double bond in the carbon chain of the fatty acid. In Omega-3 fatty acids, the first double bond is therefore in the third position, in Omega-6 fatty acids in the sixth, and in Omega-9 fatty acids (olive oil, avocados, almonds) in the ninth position. Foods rich in Omega-3 fatty acids include walnuts, flaxseeds, canola oil, and soy products. Hemp and flax oil unfortunately have a very strong taste, so I'm very sparing in the amount I use. When I make salad dressing, I use a larger proportion of olive oil and then mix in a little flax or hemp oil.

QUINOA

Quinoa, which is known as the Incan grain, originated in Peru and still grows there in the Andes. Quinoa was a staple for the Incas and was considered to be a source of life. This is not surprising as it contains large amounts of minerals and protein, including the amino acids lysine and isoleucine. The high proportion of manganese acts as an antioxidant, thus protecting us from harmful environmental effects.

36

Quinoa also provides us with plant chemicals such as ferulic acid, which chemically resembles the curcumin of turmeric. Ferulic acid is rich in the polyphenols quercetin and kaempherol. Furthermore, it is rich in polysaccharides and contains high amounts of phosphorus and copper, which are good for bone health. The Food and Agriculture Organization of the United Nations has declared the year 2013 to be the Year of Quinoa as it is a highly nutritional food. Regardless, quinoa simply tastes delicious and can be prepared quickly.

RESVERATROL

Resveratrol is found in large quantities in red grapes, red wine, and Japanese knotweed. There are several studies that point to resveratrol's life-extending effects. Since alcohol is off-limits during the 30 days, you can occasionally have a few red grapes for a snack—they are especially refreshing ice cold!

CHOCOLATE

It is no wonder that the Aztecs drank a lot of cocoa as it contains a large amount of polyphenols (about 300 different substances) and theobromine, which acts as a mood-enhancer. Theobromine is the reason why people say that chocolate makes you happy. In addition, cocoa contains N-phenylpropenoyl-L-amino acid amides (better known by the name CocoHeal), a substance that has a positive effect on the growth of skin cells. When you buy cocoa, make sure that it is high quality. I only buy unsweetened cocoa powder that has been highly de-oiled. The Challenger Chocolate (For recipe, see p. 186) is an optimal mix of ingredients. In comparison, milk chocolate contains a lot of industrial sugar, animal fats, and very little cocoa.

SOY PRODUCTS

Scientists say that soy products are capable of preventing various types of cancer such as breast and prostate cancer because they are rich in isoflavonoids, including genistein and daidzein. In Europe, you should always buy organic grade soy products as that is the only way of guaranteeing that no rainforest was cleared for cultivation. I am a fan of organic tofu because it agrees with most people and contains a high amount of calcium and protein, but only a small amount of fat. Many people complain of bloating after drinking certain soy milks—for them, I strongly recommend other kinds of plant-based milk such as oat milk.

TOMATOES

Tomatoes contain a lot of lycopene, a molecule which belongs to the carotenoid family and is responsible for the red color of tomatoes. Scientists say that of all the carotenoids, lycopene has the strongest anti-cancer effects and it helps fight agaisnt prostate cancer among others. Products such as tomato paste and sun-dried tomatoes are especially high in lycopene. Consuming tomato products together with high-quality oils potentiates the effect of lycopene.

CITRUS FRUITS

Citrus fruits contain not only very high levels of Vitamin C and terpenes, but also flavanones, a subgroup of polyphenols. Among other names, hesperidin is known as Vitamin P. Flavanones have an anti-inflammatory effect. Citrus peel is particularly rich in these substances. For lemon or orange flavor, I use only the finely grated peel of organic fruits. This way, you can "recreate" the natural and healthy taste of lemonade.

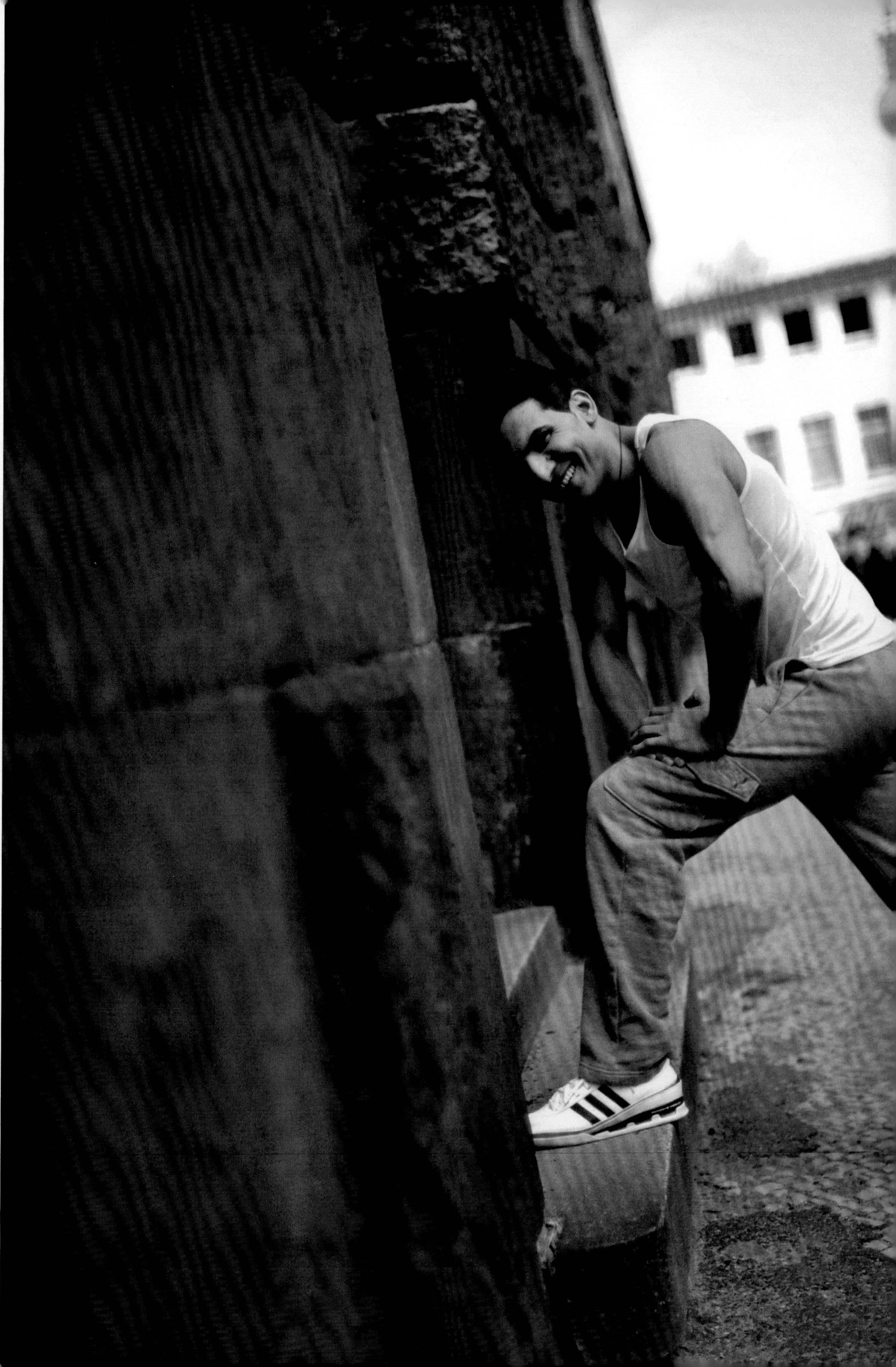

WELL PREPARED
FROM THE BEGINNING

The 30-Day Challenge—success depends a lot on good preparation. Start early with a short checklist: for the first recipes, buy non-perishable basic ingredients at an organic grocery store or supermarket with an organic section, order matcha and maybe workout clothes if you need them, and find a new bike or running shoes. Preparing yourself mentally is also important! And buying groceries is obviously just as big a part of it as reading this book.

However, this doesn't mean that your overwhelming desire to start right away has to be put on the back burner. You can, for example, already start riding your bike and perhaps eat a falafel instead of a gyro.

THE FIRST STEP: DECIDE ON YOUR GOALS

Take the time to scan your current physical and mental state and to think about whether or not you want to continue to live in the condition you are in. Part of this is opening your eyes to the harsh reality: are you overweight, lethargic, out-of-shape, or frustrated with life? If so, now is the time to take control. Today, I know that people can achieve almost anything, even if they've only experienced failure in the past. I am not in favor of realistic goals because they are too easy to achieve. Ambitious goals are much more motivating. After all, we only have one life to live. Strive to bring out the best in yourself during the Challenge, the best that you can imagine! Give everything to achieve everything! Think about what level of health and fitness you would most like to have, how many pounds of fat you would like to lose, or how much muscle mass you would like to build up. Think the unthinkable to the end: perhaps this is a half-marathon next year, a short-distance run, or even a long-distance triathlon. One of the most important basic rules for the next 30 days is to set really challenging goals. And when doing so, you can go a bit overboard. If you don't achieve your goals in 30 days, you can do so in 60 or 90. When the first 30 days have come to an end, it will be easy for you to continue the Challenge. You will once again be capable of keeping the agreements you make with yourself, without doubting yourself.

RECORD ALL THE IMPORTANT INFORMATION

Before you start, you should record your exact measurements and take your before photos—best from head to toe and in underwear. And don't worry about it if you look a little overweight in these pictures. They'll motivate you later because it's a totally amazing feeling when you get closer to your ideal body and the before pictures are just a shadow of your past. An audience of millions have seen my overweight before pictures on television programs, and instead of feeling shame, I felt proud because I had achieved something that I and others had thought was impossible.

Then you still need to take all of the important measurements—waist, hips, thighs, calves, chest, and biceps. For this, you can use a simple measuring tape. Then you need to muster all of your courage and step on to the scales naked and measure your body fat percentage. This is best done in a gym that offers initial tests when you join or with an analytical scale at home.

It's enough for you to take your measurements and pictures at the beginning and at the end of the 30 days, preferably in the same way as the first. Starting from the beginning of the Challenge, you should only weigh yourself every five to seven days, and this should be done as soon as possible after getting up. Another good way for you to check on your progress is to wrap that measuring tape around your stomach once in a while. Incidentally, consuming too much salt can throw off the next day's weight considerably.

SCHEDULE AND SHOPPING

Before you start to cook the recipes, you need high-quality organic ingredients. Look on the internet to find out where the nearest organic grocery store or supermarket that sells organic food is. Fresh, crisp ingredients are a must-have during the next 30 days—and even if you usually don't buy organic products, it's really beneficial to try to do so during the Challenge. It's best to take *Vegan for Fit* with you to the store. Or go to the publisher's website, where you can find a convenient shopping list to print out. My advice: buy fresh foods at least every three days. Many of the Vegan for Fit recipes can be easily prepared the evening before. Nevertheless, you will need to schedule some time in to cook. Processed foods, microwave dishes, and junk food are taboo.

It is essential that you figure out when you can work out. I prefer to work out in the evenings. Daily training is not required; getting a healthy amount of exercise is what matters. If you ride your bike to college, school, or the office—then you've already got one training session in. After work, you could add in a quick 30 minutes in the pool or do the Challenger exercise course (see pp. 222–229) on the way home—then you've got your second session in.

EQUIP YOURSELF

The success of some of the recipes does depend on the quality of the equipment. If you want to play it safe and save yourself some frustration, then let the following list of products serve as your guide. By the way: it's not about product placement—none of the manufacturers had any say about the items on this list.

VITAMIX BLENDER

It has two horsepower and a unique patent as it has a tamper as part of the lid that allows you to push the ingredients back into the center where the blades are. With other blenders, you always have to turn the machine off in order to scrape everything from the sides. The Vitamix has become something I can't do without in my kitchen: it makes the filling for my coffee cake unbelievably creamy. And only with this blender can I create my different variations of ice cream and even make nut butters. I recommend you buy this blender: it has a long warranty, a lot of power, and excellent results! This powerhouse is, however, not at all quiet. You can find out more about the Vitamix on the internet at www.vitamix.com/Home. It's an investment, but for your money, you'll get two horsepower, an 84-month warranty, and all the home-made cashew ice cream you want—it's the fastest and probably healthiest ice cream in the world!.

VEGETABLE PASTA CUTTER

Currently, there are two products with which you can make crisp zucchini pasta: first the hand spiral cutter from GEFU (about 20 euros in Europe or $30.00 in the U.S.), which is good when you are on the go or for use at the office, and then the more sophisticated product from Lurch (25 euros in Europe), which makes very uniform zucchini spaghetti and wide-ribbon noodles. In the United States, the tri-blade plastic spiral vegetable cutter from Paderno World Cuisine (about $30.00 on www.amazon.com) is very similar to the product made by Lurch. For wide-ribbon noodles, I use my favorite peeler, the "Gourmet" vegetable peeler by WMF, which sells for just under 8 euros in Europe and about $13.00 in the United States. A V-slicer (about 40 euros in Germany or $36.00 in the U.S.) is the best for zucchini lasagna—but be careful with your fingers, this thing is really sharp!

DEHYDRATOR

In Germany, the dehydrator used to be called a "food dryer," and it is really one of the coolest kitchen appliances. At 42°C, the enzymes that are important for digestion and our entire organism begin to die. The dehydrator dries the food and ensures that the enzymes remain intact—however, that doesn't keep me from sometimes cranking the thing up to 68°C. It resembles an oven, you have multiple baking sheets to work with, and you can dry delicious zucchini or apple chips overnight—perfect for an evening with friends or for the Challenge pizza crust. The pizza crust and crackers in *Vegan for Fit* also work in an oven, but an oven uses a lot more energy. So, it's possible without a dehydrator, but I love mine. Recommendation: buy a Sedona or an Excalibur. They both have several heating areas, a timer, and a temperature display and they can be found at a reasonable price.

SALAD SPINNER

For crisp salads that don't taste watery, you need a good salad spinner. You can find a good one starting as low as 15 euros or $20.00, and you will soon not want to do without.

ELECTRONIC KITCHEN SCALE

My recipes are weighed precisely, so sometimes the measurements used in the cookbook seem a little funny. But what really counts is the result and not one round number. I promise you that it is worth it to buy an electronic scale. You'll have so much more fun cooking the recipes because it is much faster than weighing the ingredients manually. It is super accurate—and the results speak for themselves.

KNIFE

A high-quality knife is indispensable in the kitchen. Sometimes when I go on a television cooking show, they set a blunt dagger in front of me. So, I always bring my knife with me. Bad knives are an unnecessary waste of time—and it isn't any fun to try to cut with them. For myself, I prefer all-rounders: they aren't too big and you can use them to peel onions and chop herbs. The best thing to do is to go to a store, let the people there advise you, and then invest some cash. There are some very good knives from Japan, and the best kitchen knives are handmade. It is said that at some point, you'll become one with your knife.

QUICK START

To ensure success, it is important to spend a little time preparing. Here is a short overview of the most important steps to take:

1. Define your goals. What do you want to achieve? Write down your goals!

2. Write down your starting weight and the most important measurements (waist, hips, thighs, calves, chest, and biceps), and take a picture of yourself that captures your body—from head to foot, everything should be visible.

3. If you are uncertain about your current health condition, first go to your doctor for a blood test and, if advised, an EKG or an exercise stress test.

4. You don't need to do any type of training before starting the program. It doesn't matter what shape you're in: you can start now—even if you just walk around the block at your own pace or swim the first lap that you've swam at the pool in years. Starting slow and then building up is the key to success. And you don't need to be ashamed of your current figure. We will reach your goal of having a dream body together; there is no reason to worry! Every step that you take and every lap that you swim is better than the time that you would have wasted on the couch in front of the television doing nothing.

5. Register on Facebook under www.facebook.com/groups/vegansforfitworldwide and connect with me and with other Challengers.

6. Set a definite start date for yourself. Tomorrow is better than the day after tomorrow. The start date shouldn't fall during a vacation or a business trip because it might be more difficult to eat vegan and exercise when you are away from home.

7. Decide on the recipes you want to make for the first three days—Level 2 recipes until 4:00 p.m., Level 1 recipes until 7:00 p.m., and nothing after 7:00 p.m.!

8. Find the closest store that sells organic food and purchase the ingredients you'll need for these three days.

9. Order organic matcha green tea from Aiya or from another tea shop on the internet such as "TeaGschwender"—matcha tea makes you feel like you can fly through the day.

10. Get some workout clothes. Jogging pants, a jacket, and a shirt will be enough at the beginning. The most important thing is that they're comfortable. It's essential to have good shoes if you plan on going jogging. A rain jacket and an exercise bag are also good ideas.

11. Dig your bike out of the basement and make sure it is in good working order or maybe buy yourself a fancy new one. Bike riding is the best thing that you can do to burn fat and help the environment. .

12. If you want to swim, find out where the nearest swimming pool is.

13. Would you like to build up muscle? Then find a gym and sign up—that's a good investment for your health. Alternatively, you can decide on an outside exercise course near your home to use during the Challenge. (See pp. 222–229).

14. Read the pages that cover nutrition and shopping basics (See pp. 230–231).

15. For the first day, prepare the recipes the night before or early in the morning.

16. Free yourself of everything that is holding you back: turn off the TV and instead take these 30 days to really get ahead once and for all. Maybe you will want to make a list of the things that you have wanted to do for a long time: clean out the basement or a closet, finish your taxes, renovate...

3 ... 2 ... 1 ... GO! YOUR JOURNEY CAN BEGIN!
HERE ARE THE BASIC RULES FOR YOUR CHALLENGE ONE MORE TIME:

- From the time you get up until 4:00 p.m., you may eat all Level 2 dishes and from 4:00 p.m. until 7:00 p.m. only Level 1 dishes. And after 7:00 p.m., you shouldn't eat anything.
- The important thing to remember is that after 4:00 p.m. only Level 1 and nothing after 7:00 p.m.
- For calories, follow this general guideline: as few as possible, but as many as necessary.
- You have to have a good reason to reward yourself: during the Challenge, the good reason is when you have just exercised.
- If you do sin once, stick with the program for three more days.
- Only weigh yourself once every five to seven days!
- Sleeping problems often disappear on their own once you start exercising. A short nap in the afternoon does wonders and gives you energy for the second half of the day.

A TYPICAL DAY:

Breakfast: Amaranth Yogurt Pop (Level 2)
Lunch: Mediterranean Spartan Millet Dish (Level 2)
Dinner: Zucchini Lasagna Bolognese (Level 1)

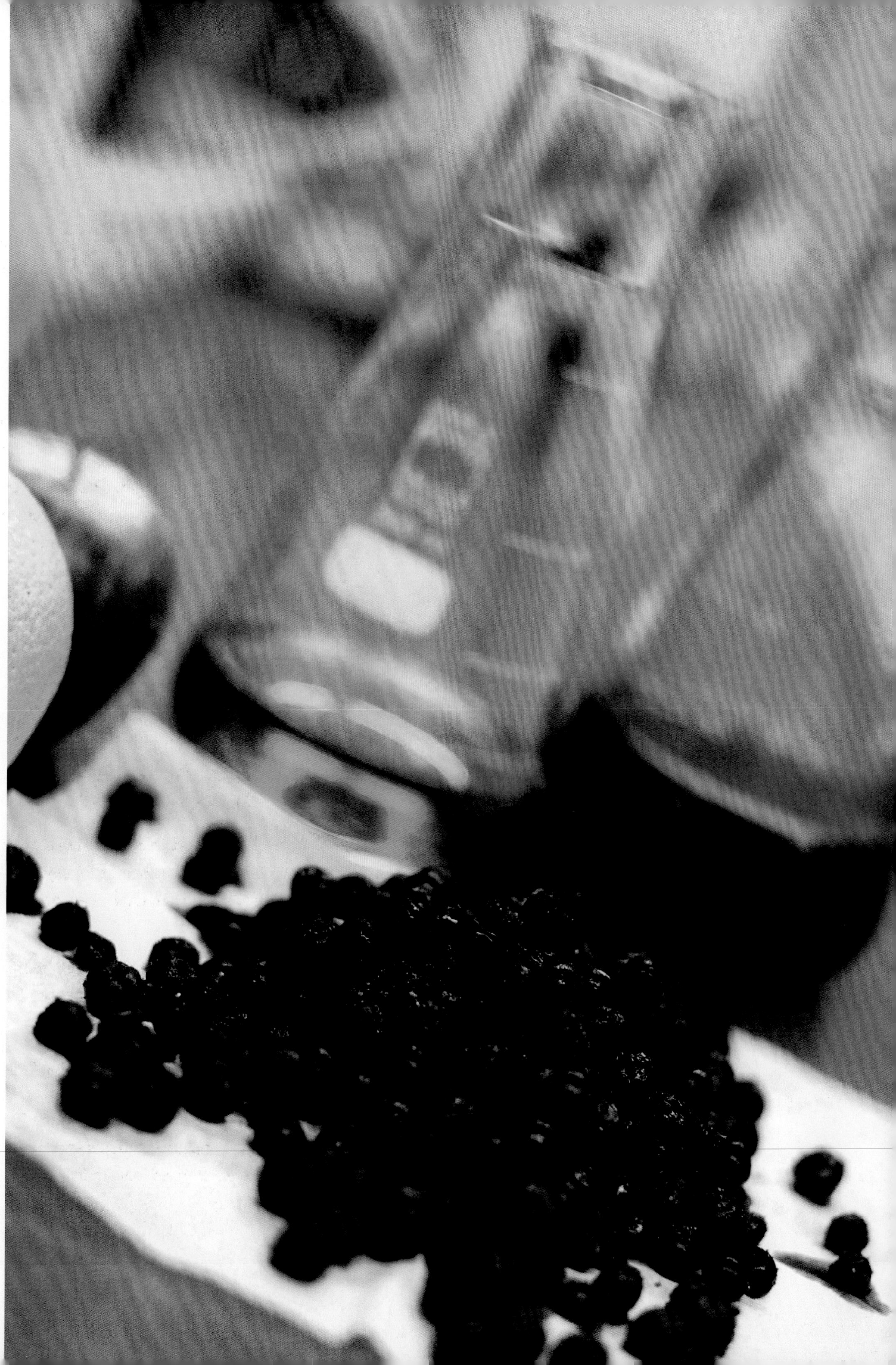

Fluids: approx. 8–12 cups (2–3 liters) non-carbonated mineral water (carbonated mineral water makes the body acidic and causes bloating); in addition, approx. 6 cups (1.5 liters) green tea and 2 matcha shakes (1 in the morning and 1 in the afternoon). It's best for you to test out for yourself the combination and amount of the individual ingredients and then to measure out ingredients according to your taste and physical needs.

It's especially important to test out the effects of the matcha shakes because they can end up being very different for each person. Some people feel the effects of a matcha shake the entire day, others don't feel a thing, and still others can't sleep at night.

If you want to put on muscle, simply train harder and always eat when you are hungry. Building on your training as you go, eating when you are hungry, and getting enough good sleep can easily replace any protein shake. It is not advisable to include a bulking up phase as is sometimes recommended for bodybuilders. You don't have to eat a disproportionately large amount of food if you want to quickly build up a lot of muscle.

If you "only" want to get healthier, and don't want to lose weight, then make more Level 2 recipes, eat more whole-grain products and rewards, and strive for a diet that is rich in vital substances.

If you do want to lose weight quickly, you can make Level 1 recipes exclusively and start the day with a matcha shake and some fruit, e.g., with fresh strawberries.

Getting healthy and losing weight often go hand in hand. Many aches and pains will vanish into thin air if you keep to the recipes—and at the same time you'll end up losing those pounds.

Get out of the habit of eating when you are not hungry! Many Challengers even managed to eat two instead of three meals because the high-quality ingredients kept them feeling satisfied for a long period of time. You need to once again learn to listen to your body. I often eat only two meals per day, but in between meals, I eat some fruit or a tablespoon of nut butter.

For the Challenge, counting calories is totally unnecessary. However, you shouldn't be shoveling calorie bombs in your mouth whenever you are in the mood. With 20 handfuls of trail mix, you will only lose weight if you are running a marathon!

Many recipes in this cookbook contain ingredients that are by all means high in fat, for example, nut butter. There is no caloric information for the recipes. Your body needs good fats; you will feel full and satisfied longer. Hunger attacks will disappear after two days, three days at the latest. Instead of counting calories, it is more important to make sure you are using high-quality ingredients and to listen to what your body needs. And that means that you should only eat when you are truly hungry—and then do so without a guilty conscience.

GET OUT OF BED

Breakfast can be more than a hard-boiled egg, white bread, and sausage. And the power recipes on the following pages will provide you with the strength you need for the day. Carbohydrates in the form of popped amaranth and whole grains should definitely be a part of what you eat at this time of day.

The options for breakfast at most hotels and cafes remain problematic. Often, I'm only offered fruit salad from a can or hot water for the organic green tea bags that I've brought with me. A tragedy. Those who travel a lot for work should be bold and simply insist on a vegan option. Where there is demand, something will eventually be offered to fill that demand. It's only in this way that the world can change.

RECIPES FOR THE
MORNING

MINI CRUNCH PANCAKES
WITH RASPBERRY YOGURT ICE CREAM

INGREDIENTS for 2 people
(6 pancakes)

Pancakes:

½ cup whole wheat flour (60 g)

½–⅔ cup soy milk (140 mL)

4 teaspoons agave syrup (20 g)

1 level teaspoon baking powder

1 pinch iodized sea salt

½ teaspoon ground vanilla

¾ cup popped amaranth (30 g)

Raspberry Yogurt Ice Cream:

1⅓ cups frozen raspberries (150 g)

2 tablespoons agave syrup (30 g)

⅓ cup plain soy yogurt (80 g)

In addition:

Some walnut oil

2 bananas

1¾ cups raspberries (200 g)

Some agave syrup

PREPARATION TIME: approx. 20 minutes

Whisk all ingredients together, except for the amaranth, until the batter is smooth. Fold in the amaranth. Drizzle walnut oil onto a paper towel to coat a non-stick skillet and then heat the skillet. For each pancake, pour about 1–2 tablespoons of batter into the pan and cook for 4 minutes over medium heat. Turn carefully and then cook for an additional 4 minutes. Place all the ingredients for the ice cream in a blender and mix thoroughly (an immersion blender can be used as an alternative). Peel the bananas and cut them into slices. Sort out damaged raspberries. Layer the pancakes, raspberries, and banana slices. Top with raspberry yogurt ice cream and agave syrup.

AH! "Pancakes are super quick and they give you energy for the day. For the ice cream, you actually only need an immersion blender and organic frozen raspberries. It's amazingly quick to make and just right for the morning rush. Fresh fruit, whole wheat, amaranth, and ice cream—a great start for a Challenger day."

AMARANTH YOGURT POP WITH RASPBERRIES AND TOASTED COCONUT FLAKES

INGREDIENTS for 2 people

1½ cups popped amaranth (60 g)

1–1¼ cups soy yogurt (260 g)

4 tablespoons agave syrup

1¾ cups raspberries (200 g)

2 pinches ground vanilla

⅓ cup coconut flakes (10 g)

PREPARATION TIME: approx. 10 minutes

Mix amaranth and soy yogurt and then sweeten with 2 tablespoons agave syrup. Sort out damaged raspberries. Marinate the berries in a mixture of 1 tablespoon agave syrup and vanilla. Toast the coconut flakes in a dry skillet approx. 3 minutes, until they begin to change color. Sweeten with 1 tablespoon agave syrup. Layer the berries and amaranth yogurt mixture in a glass and top with toasted coconut flakes.

AH! "This recipe quickly became the favorite of the first Challengers because it is quick to make and tastes wonderfully light and delicious!"

A. PEANUT CHOCOLATE MUESLI
B. CRANBERRY COCONUT PINEAPPLE MUESLI
C. BERRY MUESLI

A. Peanut Chocolate Muesli

INGREDIENTS for 1 person

⅔–¾ cup oat milk (170 mL)

2 tablespoons crunchy peanut
butter (30 g)

1 teaspoon organic cocoa

2 pinches ground vanilla

2 tablespoons agave syrup

1 cup muesli (100 g) (without added sugar)

1 tablespoon roasted peanuts (10 g)

1 banana

Some Vegan for Fit Chocolate
(See recipe on p. 186)

PREPARATION TIME: approx. 10 minutes

Mix oat milk with peanut butter, cocoa, vanilla, and
1½ tablespoons agave syrup in a blender. Mix in
muesli and let stand for 5 minutes. Mix peanuts with
½ tablespoon agave syrup. Peel the banana and cut
into thin slices. In a jar, make four layers, alternating
between layers of muesli and banana slices. Top with
peanuts, banana slices, and if desired, some Vegan for
Fit Chocolate shavings.

B. Cranberry Coconut Pineapple Muesli

INGREDIENTS for 1 person

1 cup muesli (100 g) (without added sugar)

¼ cup coconut milk (50 g)

2 tablespoons agave syrup (30 g)

¼ cup cranberries (40 g)

¾ cup soy yogurt (160 g)

¼ of a pineapple

⅔ cup coconut flakes (20 g)

PREPARATION TIME: approx. 10 minutes

Mix muesli with coconut milk, 5 teaspoons (25 g)
agave syrup, cranberries, and soy yogurt and then let
stand for 3 minutes. Peel the pineapple and remove
the stalk. Cut the fruit into bite-size pieces. Toast the
coconut flakes in a dry skillet for 1–2 minutes.
Place the muesli in a jar, add a layer of pineapple, and
then another layer of muesli. Top with pineapple,
coconut flakes, and 1 teaspoon (5 g) of agave syrup.

C. Berry Muesli

INGREDIENTS for 1 person

1 cup muesli (100 g) (without added sugar)

⅔ cup oat milk (160 mL)

2 pinches ground vanilla

2½ tablespoons agave syrup

¼ cup blueberries (30 g)

½ cup raspberries (60 g)

¼ cup blackberries (30 g)

1 tablespoon toasted almonds (10 g)

PREPARATION TIME: approx. 10 minutes

Mix muesli with oat milk, vanilla, and 1½ tablespoons
agave syrup, and then let stand for 5 minutes. Wash
and clean the blueberries, and allow to drain. Sort out
damaged raspberries and blackberries. Mix berries with
1 tablespoon agave syrup. Coarsely chop the almonds
and fold into the muesli.
In a jar, layer the muesli and berries, starting with muesli
and ending with fruit.

CHALLENGER BREAKFAST

INGREDIENTS for 2 people

1 medium sweet potato (440 g)

3 tablespoons olive oil

Iodized sea salt

2 scallions

1 red chili pepper

10 ounces soft plain tofu (280 g)

1 tablespoon white almond butter

4 tablespoons non-carbonated mineral water

3 ounces smoked tofu (80 g)

1 onion

4 pinches turmeric

Freshly ground black pepper

PREPARATION TIME: approx. 30 minutes

Preheat oven to 480°F (250°C). Peel sweet potatoes and cut into thin slices. Mix with 2 tablespoons olive oil and a little sea salt. Place on a baking sheet lined with parchment paper and bake on the highest rung in the oven for approx. 12–15 minutes, until the slices take on a light color. Wash the scallions and chili pepper and then cut both into thin rings. Mash tofu with a fork. Mix the almond butter with mineral water. Cut the smoked tofu into small cubes. Peel and finely chop the onion. Heat 1 tablespoon olive oil in a skillet and fry the smoked tofu approx. 3 minutes, until it is light brown and crispy. Add the onion and turmeric and cook together for 2 minutes. Add the plain tofu and fry for 1 minute, and then add almond butter to deglaze. Mix together with sweet potatoes and season with salt and pepper. Garnish with chili and sweet onions.

AH! "If you have time, the challenger breakfast is the perfect choice: it's rich in protein and vital substances that have long-chain carbohydrates and lots of vitamins and minerals. If you cut the potatoes thinner, the cooking time will be shorter—for when you're in a hurry."

A. ROASTED ALMONDS
B. SUPERFOOD JAM
C. HAZELNUT CHOCOLATE SPREAD

A. Roasted Almonds

INGREDIENTS for 3–4 people

¾ cup dark almond butter (200 g)

2 tablespoons agave syrup (30 g)

1 level teaspoon ground cinnamon

1 level teaspoon ground vanilla

1 pinch iodized sea salt

PREPARATION TIME: approx. 2 minutes

Stir all the **ingredients** together until a creamy mixture forms.

B. Superfood Jam

INGREDIENTS for 3–4 people

1½ cups blueberries (210 g)

⅓ cup goji berries (40 g)

6½ tablespoons agave syrup (100 g)

½ teaspoon agar agar

PREPARATION TIME: approx. 8 minutes plus approx. 40 minutes time to cool

Wash and dry **blueberries**, sorting out any damaged berries. Purée with the **goji berries, agave syrup,** and **agar agar.** In a small saucepan, bring to a boil. While stirring, allow to boil for approx. 30 seconds. Pour into a jar, let cool, and then let stand in the refrigerator for about 30 minutes.

The jam can be kept in the refrigerator for 2 days. In sterile jars, it can be stored a little longer.

C. Hazelnut Chocolate Spread

INGREDIENTS for 3–4 people

¾ cup hazelnut butter (200 g)

1 level teaspoon ground vanilla

3 tablespoons agave syrup (45 g)

4 teaspoons organic cocoa (10 g)

1 pinch iodized sea salt

PREPARATION TIME: approx. 2 minutes

Stir all the **ingredients** together until a creamy mixture forms.

SPREAD THE MESSAGE
A. TOFU HERB QUARK
B. OLIVE BUTTER
C. ARTICHOKE CASHEW SPREAD

A. Tofu Herb Quark

INGREDIENTS for 3–4 people

½ bunch fresh parsley

14 ounces soft plain tofu (400 g)

1 tablespoon lemon juice

1½ level teaspoons iodized sea salt

Zest from ¼ untreated organic lemon

1 tablespoon sunflower oil

Freshly ground black pepper

PREPARATION TIME: approx. 8 minutes

Wash parsley, shake dry, and finely chop the leaves. Purée tofu, lemon juice, and salt well until the mixture is creamy. Mix in parsley, lemon zest, and sunflower oil and then pepper to taste.

B. Olive Butter

INGREDIENTS for 3–4 people

3½ tablespoons olive oil (50 mL)

Iodized sea salt

PREPARATION TIME: approx. 1 minute plus approx. 60 minutes to chill

Stir together olive oil and sea salt. Pour into a small bowl and place in the freezer for approx. 1 hour, until the olive oil has solidified. Spread on bread immediately and enjoy right away; otherwise the oil will melt again.

C. Artichoke Cashew Spread

INGREDIENTS for 3–4 people

1 cup artichoke hearts in oil (190 g)

⅓ cup sun-dried tomatoes in oil (40 g)

1 cup cashew butter (240 g)

5 tablespoons non-carbonated mineral water (70 mL)

Freshly ground black pepper

PREPARATION TIME: approx. 5 minutes

Allow artichoke hearts and sun-dried tomatoes to drain in a sieve. Purée with the other ingredients. Pepper to taste.

FIRESTARTER

INGREDIENTS for 1 person (1 glass)

Basic Recipe with Blueberries:

½ cup rolled oats (40 g)

½ cup popped amaranth (20 g)

1⅔ cups oat milk (400 mL)

2 pinches ground vanilla

7 teaspoons agave syrup (35 g)

2 tablespoons roasted hazelnuts (15 g)

2 tablespoons walnuts (15 g)

1 tablespoon flax seeds

4 ice cubes

¾ cup blueberries (100 g)

Variation with Banana:

1 small banana (70 g)

1½ teaspoons organic cocoa

For the Booster:

1 teaspoon guarana

or

1 teaspoon matcha

PREPARATION TIME: approx. 3 minutes

Mix all **ingredients** in a blender. If you would like, add a few **blueberries** before serving. Serve. The firestarter basic recipe can be easily varied: mix all ingredients except for the blueberries with **banana** and **cocoa**. For the extra kick in the morning, I recommend **guarana** or **matcha**—then you'll be able to fly through the day!

FAST LIFE SANDWICH

INGREDIENTS for 2 people

7 ounces smoked tofu (200 g)

2 tablespoons olive oil

Iodized sea salt

Freshly ground black pepper

½ carrot

1½ cups mixed salad greens (50 g)

¾ cup alfalfa sprouts (20 g)

1 tomato

1 avocado

4 slices of thin organic whole grain

bread (or try Vegan for Fit Burger Buns; see recipe on p. 104)

1 tablespoon cashew butter (or some olive butter, see recipe on p. 63)

PREPARATION TIME: approx. 12 minutes
Cut smoked tofu into thin slices. Heat olive oil
in a skillet and fry the tofu for about 2 minutes
on each side until crispy. Salt and pepper, and
then transfer to a plate lined with paper towels
to drain. Peel and grate carrot. Wash lettuce
and then spin dry. Wash sprouts and allow to
dry. Wash tomato and cut into thin slices. Halve
the avocado and remove the pit. Spoon out the
pulp with a spoon and cut the avocado into thin
slices. Spread cashew butter or olive butter
onto bread slices. Layer 2 slices of bread with
mixed salad greens, smoked tofu, and the other
ingredients and then place the other 2 slices
of bread on top. If you are on the go, wrap the
sandwich in parchment paper (not in foil because
that requires too much energy to produce) or put
it in a transparent lunchbox—your colleagues,
classmates, and fellow students will be jealous.

AH! "This sandwich is great if you
need something hearty right away.
You can make it quickly and it's very
rich in protein since both tofu and
sprouts contain a lot of high-quality
protein. Smoked tofu is one of the few
kinds of tofu that I also like to eat raw.
If you are really in a hurry, you can
cut it paper thin, and marinate it with
a little olive oil, salt, and pepper."

TOFU SCRAMBLE

INGREDIENTS for 2 people

14 ounces soft plain tofu (400 g)

1 tablespoon sunflower oil

½ teaspoon turmeric

1 tablespoon non-carbonated
mineral water

1½ tablespoons white almond
butter

Iodized sea salt

Freshly ground black pepper

1 whole wheat bun (e.g., Vegan for Fit
Burger Buns, see recipe on p. 104)

In addition:

Chives and tomato quarters
for garnish

PREPARATION TIME: approx. 12 minutes

Mash **tofu** with a fork. Heat **sunflower oil** in
a skillet and then fry tofu with **turmeric** for
approx. 3 minutes. Add the **mineral water** and
almond butter and season with **salt**
and **pepper.**

Cut the **whole wheat bun** in half. Serve
the scrambled tofu with some **chives** and
tomato quarters.

AH! "This dish really reminds me
of scrambled eggs. But I don't miss
the typical, intense taste of eggs
at all; I like these even better. You
just have to make sure to buy the
somewhat softer tofu (not silken
tofu)—it'll give you perfect results
every time. Turmeric provides the
characteristic color and protects
our bodies because it contains
curcumin, which is thought to
have cancerpreventing effects."

BREAKFAST CRUNCH WITH ALMOND MILK

INGREDIENTS for 2 people

Breakfast Crunch:

¾ cup popped amaranth (30 g)

1⅓ cups sugar-free cornflakes (50 g)

¾ cup rolled oats (70 g)

¼ cup roasted almonds (30 g)

⅓ cup goji berries (40 g)

¼ cup cranberries (40 g) (sweetened with apple juice)

¼ cup walnuts (30 g)

1 tablespoon flax seeds

Local seasonal fruit
(e.g., 100 g blueberries and 150 g strawberries)

Almond Milk:

¾ cup ice cubes (100 g)

3 tablespoons agave syrup (40 g)

6½ tablespoons white almond butter (100 g)

1 pinch iodized sea salt

PREPARATION TIME: approx. 7 minutes
Put all ingredients for the Breakfast Crunch, except for the fruit, into a large bowl and mix gently. Purée all ingredients for the almond milk together with 1⅔ cups (400 mL) of water in a blender. Peel or clean the fruit and then wash and cut into bite-size pieces. Put the Breakfast Crunch into bowls, serve with fruit, and pour almond milk on top.

AH! "The perfect combination of the best ingredients—a far cry from the many overly sugary cereals! The day will come when I will be able to order this mix in hotels and buy it at organic grocery stores."

APPLE CINNAMON MILLET CREAM

INGREDIENTS for 2 people

¾ cup millet (150 g)

2 cups oat milk (500 mL)

1 level teaspoon ground cinnamon

1 pinch iodized sea salt

1 tablespoon cashew butter

7 teaspoons agave syrup (35 g)

1 apple

¼ cup dried cranberries (40 g)

PREPARATION TIME: approx. 45 minutes plus about 10 minutes for cooling

Combine the **millet** and **oat milk** in a small saucepan and bring to a boil. Then reduce the heat to low and allow to simmer, partially covered, for approx. 35–40 minutes. Stir occasionally, and if necessary, add a little **oat milk**. Then add **cinnamon, sea salt, cashew butter,** and **agave syrup** to the millet, adding some **oat milk** if necessary so that the mixture cashew butter becomes creamier. Transfer to a flat container and put in the freezer for 10 minutes. Peel and core the **apple** and cut it into small pieces. Add the **cranberries** to the millet cream and serve.

AH! "Millet has been somewhat forgotten although it is rich in B vitamins and iron. It's one of the alkaline-forming grains and is even gluten free. Millet also contains silicon, which is great for your skin and hair. If you wash millet before cooking, it'll taste even better. It works best to cook the millet the night before and then to mix everything together in the morning."

CHALLENGER FRUIT BREAD

INGREDIENTS

for approx. 18 slices

3 tablespoons natural fermentation starter (20 g) or 1 pkg. organic yeast

5 cups whole grain spelt flour (550 g)

⅔ cup cranberries (100 g)

About 12 prunes (100 g)

3 tablespoons goji berries (20 g)

⅔ cup cashews (100 g)

⅔–½ cup roasted hazelnuts (50 g)

¾ cup popped amaranth (30 g)

½ cup flax seeds (50 g)

6½ tablespoons agave syrup (100 g)

½ teaspoon iodized sea salt

Oil for greasing pan

AH! "This is probably the healthiest and one of the tastiest breads in the world. The dough tastes similar to that of a sourdough bread. Natural fermentation starter can be purchased at some organic grocery stores or on the internet. Given the long rising time, you will have to have patience, but the preparation time is then short. Goji berries have the power to fight free radicals."

PREPARATION TIME: approx. 70 minutes plus about 18 hours resting time

Add just under 1½ cups (350 mL) warm water to a bowl, and then using a whisk, stir in the natural fermentation starter or yeast. Stir in 2¾ cups (300 g) of flour using a wooden spoon and dust with a little flour. Wrap the bowl in a plastic bag, leaving a small slit on the edge. Then wrap in a kitchen towel and allow to rest in a warm place at approx. 86–95°F (30–35°C) for 12 hours (30 minutes if you are using yeast).

Stir ⅔ cup (150 mL) warm water into the mixture, fold in 2¼ cups (250 g) flour using a wooden spoon, wrap the bowl as before, and allow to rest again for 5–6 hours (40 minutes if you are using yeast). The dough should now be visibly larger.

Preheat oven to 350°F (180°C). Coarsely chop the dried fruit and nuts and fold into the dough together with the amaranth, flax seeds, agave syrup, and sea salt. Put the dough into a 10-inch loaf pan (26 cm) that has been greased with oil. Bake in the middle of a hot oven at 350°F (180°C) for 60 minutes. Allow to cool before slicing, and then enjoy, perhaps with peanut butter.

BERLIN TOAST
WITH CASHEW BANANA FILLING
AND CRUNCHY OUTER LAYER

INGREDIENTS for 2 people

Berlin Toast:

¼ cup cashew butter (60 g)

½ teaspoon ground vanilla

1 pinch iodized sea salt

1 tablespoon agave syrup

4 thin slices whole grain bread

1 banana

Crunchy Outer Layer:

½ cup whole-wheat flour (60 g)

7 tablespoons soy milk (105 mL)

2 tablespoons agave syrup (30 g)

1 teaspoon ground vanilla

1 pinch iodized sea salt

½ teaspoon ground cinnamon

1 cup cornflakes (30 g)

¼ cup popped amaranth (10 g)

5 tablespoons canola oil

PREPARATION TIME: approx. 25 minutes

Stir **cashew butter** together with ½ teaspoon **vanilla, sea salt,** and **agave syrup** until creamy. Spread this cream onto **bread slices.** Peel and cut **banana** into thin slices and then arrange on 2 of the bread slices. Cover each one with a second slice of bread and press down a bit. For the outer layer, mix together **flour, soy milk,** agave syrup, vanilla, 1 pinch sea salt, and **cinnamon** using a whisk. In a wide shallow bowl, crumble the **cornflakes** with your hands and then mix together with the **popped amaranth.** Heat the **canola oil** in a skillet. Coat the outside of the sandwich with the flour batter and then with the cornflakes amaranth mixture. Over medium heat, cook the toasted sandwiches for approx. 3–4 min. on each side. In addition, cook the sandwiches on the narrow sides for a short time by standing them up on their edges. Transfer to a plate lined with paper towels to drain and use another paper towel to dab off any excess oil. Serve with fresh fruit, and if desired, with Cashew Chocolate Chip Ice Cream (For recipe, see page 191) or Attila's Whipped Cream (For recipe, see p. 185: Low-Carb Tartlets with Strawberries and Coconut Whipped Cream).

FIT ON THE GO

When you're at the office, you can take your vegetable cutter with you and quickly make yourself zucchini spaghetti—just prepare the sauce or one of the three pestos ahead of time. This option doesn't take much time and you'll feel full, but at the same time, it's so light that you won't hit a low point after the meal. If you want a crisp salad, it's best to prepare it at home in advance. At home, you can tear, wash, spin dry, and mix, but it's best to bring the salad dressing in a separate container with you to work. That way it will stay fresh. Salads can be really special: try taking the Chili Crackers and Dip with you and you'll feel full, without having sinned.

RECIPES FOR
AFTERNOONS AND EVENINGS

RECIPES FOR AFTERNOONS: LEVELS 1 AND 2—RECIPES FOR EVENINGS: ONLY LEVEL 1

MOUSSAKA RELOADED WITH "GROUND TOFU" AND CASHEW PARSLEY CREAM

INGREDIENTS for 2 people

Moussaka:

1 small sweet potato (300 g)

1 medium eggplant (270 g)

4 tablespoons olive oil

½ teaspoon iodized sea salt

7.5 ounces tofu (220 g)

1 red onion

2 garlic cloves

½ cup tomato paste (120 g)

1 teaspoon agave syrup

Freshly ground black pepper

2 tablespoons red wine (30 mL)

Cashew Parsley Cream:

2 tablespoons unsweetened cashew butter (30 g)

1 tablespoon chopped parsley

Iodized sea salt

Freshly ground black pepper

AH! "Tofu works great as a healthy, light, and protein-rich alternative to ground beef. However, you must keep the Number One Golden Rule: always fry tofu in an ample amount of oil in a skillet until it's golden brown."

PREPARATION TIME: approx. 35 minutes

Preheat oven to 480°F (250°C). Peel the sweet potato and cut into thin slices. Wash the eggplant and cut into slices just under ½ inch (about 1 cm) thick. Combine 2 tablespoons olive oil and ½ teaspoon salt. Coat the sweet potatoes and eggplant with this mixture. Bake on a baking sheet lined with parchment paper in the oven on the highest rung approx. 15 minutes, until the vegetables take on a light brown color. In the meantime, crumble the tofu. Then peel and finely chop both the onion and garlic cloves. Heat 2 tablespoons olive oil in a skillet and fry tofu approx. 4 minutes. Add the onion and garlic and sauté for an additional 3 minutes. Add the tomato paste and agave syrup and cook for 1 more minute; salt, pepper, and deglaze with red wine. Remove skillet from heat.

For the cream, heat the cashew butter with 4½ tablespoons (70 mL) of water in a small saucepan. Fold in the parsley, and season with salt and pepper. To serve, make stacks by alternately layering 1 eggplant slice, some ground tofu, 1 sweet potato slice, and some more ground tofu. Continue with this order until there are no ingredients left. Finally, pour the Cashew Parsley Cream on top.

CAULIFLOWER CURRY CRUNCH

INGREDIENTS for 2 people

1 medium-size cauliflower (1.5 kg)

Iodized sea salt

¼ cup roasted almonds (30 g)

½ cup popped amaranth (20 g)

4 tablespoons olive oil

¼ cup white almond butter (60 g)

1 teaspoon curry powder

Freshly ground black pepper

Some basil

PREPARATION TIME: approx. 15 minutes

Wash the cauliflower and then cut approx. 2.2 pounds (1 kg) of florets from the core. In a large covered saucepan, cook the cauliflower for 6 minutes in well-salted boiling water. Pour into a sieve and allow to drain. Chop the almonds. Mix together with the amaranth and 2 tablespoons olive oil. Salt.

Combine almond butter with curry powder and 6½ tablespoons (100 mL) water. Season with salt and pepper. Warm the mixture in a small saucepan, adding some water if the almond butter gets too thick.

Mix the cauliflower with 2 tablespoons olive oil and place on a plate. Sprinkle the amaranth mixture on top and pour the curry sauce over the dish. Garnish with basil.

AH! "Mark Twain once wrote, 'Cauliflower is nothing but cabbage with a college education.' I think he meant that cauliflower can do much more than plain old cabbage. And that's what the most recent scientific studies have shown as well. Cauliflower contains many substances such as glucosinolate and sulforaphane, which are believed to have cancer-preventing effects. It's also rich in vitamins, minerals, and folic acid."

CAPRESE VEGAN STYLE

INGREDIENTS for 2 people

14 ounces plain tofu (400 g)

Approx. 3 tablespoons olive oil

1 teaspoon agave syrup

1 teaspoon dried oregano

Iodized sea salt

Freshly ground black pepper

3 vine-ripened tomatoes

½ bunch basil

1 garlic clove

Grated peel of ½ organic lemon

Balsamic vinegar to sprinkle on top

PREPARATION TIME: approx. 15 minutes

Cut **tofu** into slices approx. ¼ inch (approx. ½ cm) thick and then cut into circles, perhaps using a glass. Heat 2 tablespoons **olive oil** in a skillet and fry the tofu approx. 3 minutes on each side. Add **agave syrup, oregano,** and a little **sea salt** to the pan and allow to caramelize for about 10 seconds. Transfer to a plate lined with paper towels to drain. Season with **salt** and **pepper**.

Wash **tomatoes** and cut into slices. Layer the tomatoes and tofu alternately onto a plate. Wash the **basil,** shake dry, and finely chop the leaves. Peel and finely chop the **garlic clove.** Sprinkle the basil, garlic, and **lemon peel** over the tofu and tomatoes. Sprinkle **olive oil** and **vinegar** on top. Season with **salt** and **pepper**.

AH! "For this recipe, I recommend using a somewhat softer tofu (but not silken tofu) that has more air bubbles and is a bit smoother. My publisher tried this recipe out. He transformed the tofu into the finest mozzarella by cutting it into thin slices and marinating it in hot water with a generous amount of salt, olive oil, fresh garlic, and basil leaves for 2 hours. To serve, add a splash of lemon juice and white balsamic reduction. Perfect!"

CURRY ALMOND AMARANTH
WITH ASPARAGUS IN ORANGE SAUCE

INGREDIENTS for 2 people

¾ cup amaranth (160 g) (not popped)

Iodized sea salt

¾ bunch green asparagus (370 g)

2 tablespoons olive oil

1 organic orange

1½ tablespoons white almond
butter

Freshly ground black pepper

1 red onion

2 garlic cloves

2½ tablespoons roasted almonds
(20 g)

4 sun-dried tomatoes in oil

1 teaspoon curry powder

AH! "It's best to cook the
amaranth the day before. Doing
this will drastically reduce the
preparation time."

PREPARATION TIME: approx. 50 minutes

Place amaranth in a small saucepan. Add
2¾ cups (660 mL) water and ¼ teaspoon salt
and bring to a boil. Allow to cook over medium
heat approx. 36–38 minutes, until the water is
absorbed. Stir occasionally.

Peel the asparagus and cut off the woody
ends. Heat 1 tablespoon olive oil in a skillet
and sauté the asparagus for 3 minutes over
high heat. Transfer to a plate lined with paper
towels to drain.

Wash the orange in hot water and then dry
off. Finely grate half of the peel and squeeze
the juice from the orange. Allow both to cook
together with 1 tablespoon almond butter in a
small saucepan, stirring occasionally, approx.
30 seconds until the sauce has thickened.
Season with salt and pepper.

Peel and finely chop onion and garlic cloves.
Coarsely chop almonds. Allow most of the
liquid to drain from the sun-dried tomatoes
and then finely chop. Heat 1 tablespoon olive
oil in a skillet. Sauté onion, garlic, curry
powder, and almonds approx. 2 minutes. Add
the amaranth and sun-dried tomatoes and
allow to cook for a short time. Bind the sauce
with ½ tablespoon almond butter and salt. Put
the amaranth between 2 metal rings (Diameter:
4.5 and 6 inches or 12 and 15 cm) and then
place on the plates. Put the asparagus in the
middle and then top with the sauce.

EGGPLANT BOATS MEXICAN STYLE WITH THYME ALMOND CREAM

INGREDIENTS for 2 people

Eggplant Boats:

2 eggplants (520 g)

5 tablespoons olive oil

Iodized sea salt

2 red onions (130 g after onions are peeled)

1 garlic clove

½ chili pepper

4 sun-dried tomatoes in oil

1 level teaspoon cumin

1 level teaspoon oregano

3 cups cooked kidney beans (190 g) (drained)

3½ tablespoons tomato paste (50 g)

1 teaspoon agave syrup

Freshly ground black pepper

Thyme Almond Cream:

¼ cup white almond butter (60 g)

¼ bunch thyme

AH! "Eggplants are basically fat-free, and they are rich in B Vitamins; fiber that makes us feel satisfied; and minerals such as magnesium, manganese, and potassium."

PREPARATION TIME: approx. 40 minutes

Preheat oven to 480°F (250°C). Wash and cut the eggplants in half. Carefully scrape out the eggplant flesh with a tablespoon so you are left with a shell that is a little less than ¼ inch (approx. 5 mm) wide. Finely chop the eggplant flesh. Combine 2 tablespoons olive oil and a little salt and use this mixture to coat the eggplant halves that have been scooped out. Place on a baking sheet lined with parchment paper and bake on the highest rung in the oven for approx. 17 minutes, until they take on a light color.

In the meantime, peel and finely chop the onions and garlic clove. Remove the core and membranes from the chili pepper. Wash and finely chop the chili pepper. Allow most of the liquid to drain from the sun-dried tomatoes and then finely chop.

Heat 2 tablespoons olive oil in a skillet and sauté onions, chili pepper, garlic, and cumin approx. 2 min. Add eggplant flesh, oregano, and tomatoes and sauté approx. 5 minutes, stirring occasionally. Stir in kidney beans, tomato paste, and agave syrup. Season with salt and pepper.

For the cream, combine almond butter and just under 3 tablespoons (40 mL) water. Wash the thyme and shake dry. Finely chop the leaves and fold into the almond cream.

Remove the eggplant halves from the oven, fill with the contents from the pan, and pour the cream on top. Bake the eggplant boats for about 8 additional minutes at 480°F (250°C), until a crisp surface forms. If you like, drizzle a little olive oil on top and then serve.

MEDITERRANEAN SPARTAN MILLET

INGREDIENTS for 2 people

1¼ cups millet (250 g)

3½ cups non-carbonated mineral
water (850 mL)

Iodized sea salt

1 onion

1 zucchini

½ eggplant

1 carrot

Approx. 4 tablespoons olive oil

⅓ cup tomato paste (80 g)

2 teaspoons oregano

Freshly ground black pepper

⅓ cup Sango Radish Sprouts (30 g)
(or alfalfa sprouts)

⅓ cup roasted hazelnuts (40 g)

PREPARATION TIME: approx. 30 minutes
Place **millet, mineral water,** and ½ teaspoon
salt in a small saucepan. Bring to a boil and
then allow to cook over medium heat approx.
22 minutes, stirring occasionally.
Peel and finely chop the **onion.** Wash the
zucchini and **eggplant** and cut into small
cubes. Peel the **carrot,** cut it lengthwise, and
slice. Heat 3 tablespoons **olive oil** in a skillet
and sauté vegetables for 5 minutes. Next add
the **tomato paste** and **oregano,** and cook
approx. 1 minute while stirring. Season with
salt and pepper. Mix in the millet. **Salt** and
pepper again.
Wash the **sprouts** and allow them to drain.
Coarsely chop the **hazelnuts.** Serve this
Spartan dish on wooden plates and top with
hazelnuts, sprouts, and a liberal drizzle of
olive oil.

AH! "The Spartan way of life that
this recipe is named for was simple.
The Spartans had a disciplined and
decisive attitude about themselves
and life—a good model for us
during the Challenge."

**PUMPKIN FRIES
WITH 3 DIPS**

INGREDIENTS for 2 people

Pumpkin Fries:

1 small Hokkaido pumpkin (750 g)

1 level teaspoon freshly chopped
rosemary leaves

3 tablespoons olive oil

½ teaspoon paprika

1 level teaspoon gyros seasoning

1 level teaspoon iodized sea salt

Pea Yogurt Dip:

1⅔ cups frozen peas (200 g)

Iodized sea salt

1 red onion

1 tablespoon olive oil

1 teaspoon curry powder

Grated peel of ½ organic
lemon

⅔ cup plain soy yogurt (150 g)

Avocado Blood Orange Dip:

2 avocados

1 organic blood orange

Iodized sea salt

Basil Ketchup:

1 white onion

1 garlic clove

About 23 cherry tomatoes (350 g)

½ bunch basil

2 sun-dried tomatoes in oil

3 tablespoons olive oil

2 tablespoons white wine vinegar

2 rounded tablespoons tomato
paste

1 level teaspoon iodized sea salt

1 tablespoon agave syrup

AH! "Don't cut the fries too thick and
make sure to take them out of the
oven when they turn golden brown.
Then they'll be nice and crispy."

PREPARATION TIME: approx. 25 minutes

Preheat oven to 480°F (250°C).

Wash the pumpkin. Cut it in half and then scoop out the
seeds with a tablespoon. Cut the pumpkin into quarters and
use a sharp knife to cut into fries. Mix all other ingredients
together with the pumpkin. Distribute evenly onto a baking
sheet lined with parchment paper and bake on the highest
rung in the oven for approx. 15–17 minutes, until the fries are
golden brown. Put the Hokkaido fries into cones made out of
parchment paper and serve with dip.

PREPARATION TIME PER DIP: approx. 15 minutes

Pea Yogurt Dip

For the Pea Yogurt Dip, cook the peas in well-salted boiling
water with a little salt approx. 3 minutes and then drain. Peel
and finely chop the onion. Heat olive oil in a skillet and cook
onion with curry powder for 3 minutes. Coarsely purée ¾ of
the peas with the lemon peel in a tall, narrow container. Mix
in the soy yogurt, the remaining peas, and the curry onions.
Season with salt.

Avocado Blood Orange Dip

For the Avocado Blood Orange Dip, halve the avocados and
remove the pits. With a tablespoon, scoop out the pulp and
place it in a bowl. Wash the blood orange with hot water, dry
it off, and finely grate ¼ of the peel. Squeeze 3 tablespoons
of juice from the orange. Purée the juice and peel with the
avocado in a blender. Season with salt.

Basil Ketchup

For the ketchup, peel and finely chop the onion and garlic.
Wash and halve the cherry tomatoes. Wash the basil, shake
dry, and finely chop the leaves. Allow most of the liquid to
drain from the sun-dried tomatoes and then finely chop.
Heat olive oil in a skillet and cook onion and garlic approx.
3 minutes. Add the cherry tomatoes and cook approx.
6 minutes, while stirring. Remove from heat and purée with
white wine vinegar, tomato paste, salt, and agave syrup.
If desired, season with salt. Fold in basil and sun-dried
tomatoes and put in the refrigerator to cool.

CARBONARA SPAGHETTI WITH ZUCCHINI NOODLES

INGREDIENTS for 2 people

6½ tablespoons white almond butter (100 g)

½ bunch parsley

5.5 ounces smoked tofu (160 g)

1 onion (120 g after onion is peeled)

1 garlic clove

Approx. 5 tablespoons olive oil

Grated peel of ½ organic lemon

1 teaspoon lemon juice

Iodized sea salt

Freshly ground black pepper

5 medium-size zucchini (approx. 1 kg)

AH! "This is a dream come true since 1 small zucchini (100 g) only has 19 calories. The same amount of noodles has 362 calories. So you could eat 19 times more zucchini pasta and still consume the same number of calories. No one would do this, but it does make the point clear that you really can't get fat from eating zucchini noodles. And with a tasty sauce, these 'noodles' are simply delicious—you don't even notice that you are 'just' crunching on vegetables. The spiral cutter is available online or in specialty shops for a reasonable price."

PREPARATION TIME: approx. 25 minutes

Mix **almond butter** and one cup (240 mL) water using a whisk. Wash the parsley, shake dry, and finely chop the leaves. Cut the **smoked tofu** into small cubes. Peel and finely chop both the **onion** and the **garlic clove**. Heat 2 tablespoons **olive oil** in a skillet and fry the smoked tofu approx. 3 minutes. Add the onion and garlic and cook for an additional 3 minutes. Add the almond butter mixture, **lemon peel, lemon juice,** and parsley. Season liberally with **salt** and **pepper.** Allow the carbonara to come just to a boil and thicken. Wash the **zucchini** and make spaghetti using a spiral vegetable cutter. Toss the zucchini spaghetti with 2 tablespoons **olive oil** and a little **sea salt.** Fold into the hot sauce and heat for 1 minute. Serve in deep pasta dishes, drizzle some **olive oil** on top, and grind fresh **pepper** over everything.

BOLOGNESE SPAGHETTI WITH ZUCCHINI NOODLES AND ALMOND PARMESAN TOPPING

INGREDIENTS for 2 people

10 ounces firm plain tofu (280 g)

2 onions

2 garlic cloves

6 sun-dried tomatoes in oil

½ bunch basil

Approx. 9 tablespoons olive oil

2–3 teaspoons dried oregano

Iodized sea salt

Freshly ground black pepper

¾ cup tomato paste (200 g)

2 teaspoons agave syrup

⅓ cup red wine (80 mL)

Approx. 5 medium-size zucchini (about 1 kg)

½ cup roasted almonds (60 g)

PREPARATION TIME: approx. 15 minutes

In a bowl, mash the tofu with a fork. Peel and finely chop both the onions and garlic cloves. Allow the sun-dried tomatoes to drain and then finely chop. Wash the basil, shake dry, and finely chop the leaves. Heat 6 tablespoons olive oil in a skillet and fry the tofu approx. 4 minutes while stirring, until it takes on a light golden brown color. Add the onions, garlic, and oregano and then cook for an additional 4 minutes. Season with salt and pepper. Add the tomato paste, sun-dried tomatoes, and agave syrup, and allow everything to caramelize for 1 minute. Deglaze with red wine and allow to cook for 1 minute. Fold in the basil. Season with salt and pepper. Wash the zucchini and make spaghetti using a spiral vegetable cutter. Toss the zucchini spaghetti with 2 tablespoons olive oil and a little sea salt. Carefully fold into the hot sauce and allow to heat for 1 minute.

Coarsely grind roasted almonds with 2 pinches of salt in a blender until the mixture looks like parmesan.

Serve in deep pasta dishes. Top with almond parmesan and a little olive oil.

RED ROCKET
ROASTED BELL PEPPERS STUFFED WITH LENTILS AND BUTTERNUT SQUASH WITH CASHEW SAFFRON FROTH

INGREDIENTS for 2 people

Roasted Bell Peppers:

1 tablespoon olive oil

Iodized sea salt

2 red bell peppers

Pumpkin Lentil Filling:

½ bunch thyme

About ½ butternut squash (470 g)
(alternatively Hokkaido pumpkin)

4 tablespoons olive oil

Iodized sea salt

1 onion

2 pinches turmeric

1⅓ cups cooked green lentils (100 g)
(drained)

Freshly ground black pepper

Cashew Saffron Froth:

3 tablespoons unsweetened cashew

butter (50 g)

A few saffron threads

Grated peel of ¼ organic lemon

1 teaspoon freshly pressed lemon juice

Iodized sea salt

AH! "Bell peppers contain more Vitamin C than lemons and they smell great when they are roasted in the oven—two more reasons to eat them more often. For bell peppers, it is especially important that you buy organic because conventional bell peppers are one of the types of conventional vegetables that often have high levels of pesticide residues."

PREPARATION TIME: approx. 35 minutes

Preheat oven to approx. 480°F (250°C). Combine olive oil and approx. 2 pinches of salt. Wash bell peppers and brush them with oil.

For the filling, wash the thyme and shake dry. Then strip off approx. 1 tablespoon of leaves. Peel the squash, remove the seeds (If using Hokkaido pumpkin, wash, but do not peel.), and cut into about 1 inch (2.4 cm) vertical strips. Mix with 2 tablespoons olive oil, thyme, and 1 pinch sea salt. Place bell peppers and squash on a baking sheet lined with parchment paper and bake approx. 20 minutes, until the slices take on a light color. Then allow to cool for a short while.

Heat 2 tablespoons olive oil in a skillet. Peel and finely chop onion and sauté in the oil with turmeric approx. 3 minutes, until onion becomes translucent.

Coarsely chop squash with a knife and place in a bowl. Add lentils and onions. Season with salt and pepper. Use a sharp knife to cut the top off of each of the bell peppers, and then use a teaspoon to carefully remove seeds and membranes. Place the bell peppers upside down on the parchment paper so that any fluid can drain out. Then fill with the lentil squash mixture.

For the Cashew Saffron Froth, purée ⅔ cup (160 mL) water, cashew butter, saffron, lemon peel, and lemon juice in a small saucepan. Bring to a boil while stirring. Season with sea salt and then use an immersion blender to make the mixture frothy.

PARSNIP RISOTTO
WITH SUGAR SNAP PEAS

INGREDIENTS for 2 people

Iodized sea salt

¾ cup sugar snap peas (160 g)

Approx. 6 tablespoons olive oil

¼ cup almonds (30 g)

4–5 parsnips (560 g) (alternatively carrots)

2 red onions

2 garlic cloves

8 sun-dried tomatoes in oil

⅓ cup white wine (80 mL)

2 tablespoons white almond butter

Freshly ground black pepper

AH! "The 340 calories in 100 g of uncooked white rice add up really quickly. The same amount of parsnips, on the other hand, has only 21 calories and a large amount of vital substances and vitamins and minerals. Simply grate the parsnips and then chop them so that the pieces are about the size of grains of rice. Then you can use the parsnips just like you would 'rice'."

PREPARATION TIME: approx. 20 minutes

In a small saucepan, bring a little more than an inch (approx. 3 cm) of water to a boil and add a little **salt**. In the meantime, wash the **sugar snap peas** and cut off the ends. Cut the peas lengthwise in fine strips and cook in the well-salted boiling water approx. 2–3 minutes. Drain in a sieve. Heat 1 tablespoon olive oil in a skillet and sauté peas approx. 1 minute. Season with **salt**. Toast the **almonds** in a dry pan approx. 3 minutes; then coarsely chop them. Peel and coarsely grate the **parsnips.** Then chop the parsnip pieces with a knife until they are about the size of grains of rice. Peel and finely chop the **onions** and **garlic cloves.** Allow the **sun-dried tomatoes** to drain a little. First cut lengthwise and then crosswise into fine strips. Heat 4 tablespoons **olive oil** in a skillet and sauté onions and garlic for approx. 2 minutes. Add the **white wine,** tomatoes, sugar snap peas, and parsnips and cook everything together for 1 minute while stirring. Fold in the **almond butter** and season with **salt** and **pepper.** Place the Parsnip Risotto in bowls, sprinkle almonds over the dish, and drizzle **olive oil** on top.

TOFU BURGERS WITH AVOCADO CREAM
AND CHILI KETCHUP

(For recipe, see page 105)

VEGAN FOR FIT BURGER BUNS

INGREDIENTS

for approx. 8 buns

4½ cups whole grain spelt flour (500 g)

1⅔ cups non-carbonated mineral water (390 mL)

1½ tablespoons agave syrup

1 pkg. organic yeast

1 cup popped amaranth (40 g)

1½ tablespoons white almond butter (20 g)

1 teaspoon iodized sea salt

⅓ cup light sesame seeds (45 g)

AH! "The tofu burger mixture may be a little drier or wetter each time, depending on the water content of the bell pepper. The important thing here is that you really mix everything together well. You can also add a little water until the mixture has just the right consistency and isn't crumbly. The locust bean gum in the recipe does a great job of holding the mixture together—even on the grill. If you are barbecuing, you should brush the burgers with some oil first, and then grill on each side for approx. 5 minutes."

PREPARATION TIME: approx. 25 minutes plus approx. 100 minutes resting time

Put **flour** in a large bowl and make a well in the center. Pour just over 3 tablespoons (50 mL) **mineral water, agave syrup,** and **yeast** into the well and stir these together. Allow to rest for 30 minutes. Then add just under 1½ cups (340 mL) warm mineral water and knead everything into a smooth dough. Dust with some flour and cover the bowl with a kitchen towel. Allow to rest in a warm place for 40 minutes. Then knead in the **popped amaranth, almond butter,** and **sea salt** and form into buns. Place on a baking sheet lined with parchment paper and cover. Allow to rise for 30 minutes.

Preheat oven to 350°F (180°C). Brush the buns with a little water and sprinkle the **sesame seeds** on top. Bake in the middle of the oven for 20 minutes.

TOFU BURGERS WITH AVOCADO CREAM AND CHILI KETCHUP

(Photo on page 102)

INGREDIENTS for 6 burgers

Tofu Burgers:

10.5 ounces firm plain tofu (300 g)

2 red onions

1 red bell pepper

4 tablespoons olive oil

½ cup whole wheat breadcrumbs (60 g)

2 teaspoons medium-hot mustard

3 teaspoons hot paprika

2 teaspoons locust bean gum (If not available, you can use guar gum.)

1½ teaspoons iodized sea salt

Freshly ground black pepper

Chili Ketchup:

⅓ cup tomato paste (90 g)

1 level teaspoon iodized sea salt

1 tablespoon lemon juice

½ tablespoon agave syrup

Grated peel of ¼ organic lemon

1 pinch chili

Avocado Cream:

½ bunch basil

2 avocados

1 tablespoon lemon juice

1 teaspoon cashew butter

Iodized sea salt

Freshly ground black pepper

In addition:

Mixed greens

2 onions

½ cucumber

4 tomatoes

6 Vegan for Fit Burger Buns (For recipe, see page 104)

PREPARATION TIME: approx. 30 minutes

For the burgers, mash the tofu with a fork. Peel and finely chop the onions. Halve the bell pepper, remove the seeds, wash, and finely chop. Heat 2 tablespoons olive oil in a skillet and sauté onions and bell pepper approx. 5 minutes. Mix the contents of the pan together with the tofu, breadcrumbs, mustard, 3 tablespoons water, paprika, locust bean gum, and salt and then form the burgers from this mixture. Season with pepper. Over medium heat, fry the burgers in 2 tablespoons of hot oil approx. 4 minutes on each side. Transfer to a plate lined with paper towels to drain.

For the Chili Ketchup, combine all ingredients in a bowl. For the Avocado Cream, wash the basil and shake it dry. Finely chop the leaves. Halve the avocado and remove the pit. Spoon out the pulp with a tablespoon. Purée the avocado with the lemon juice and cashew butter or mash these together with a fork. Fold in the basil and season with salt and pepper. Wash the mixed greens and spin dry. Peel the onions and cut into rings. Wash the cucumber and tomatoes and cut both into slices. On one half of each bun, spread a layer of Chili Ketchup. Then add the mixed greens, Tofu Burger, Avocado Basil Cream, onion rings, and cucumber and tomato slices. Put the other half of the bun on top. An ice-cold matcha shake (For recipe, see page 202) and pumpkin fries (For recipe, see page 93) taste great with these burgers.

LOW-CARB MAKI SUSHI

INGREDIENTS

for about 2 people

(2 sushi rolls)

7 ounces firm plain tofu (200 g)

3 tablespoons canola oil

3 tablespoons soy sauce (40 mL)

2½ tablespoons agave syrup

3 tablespoons dark tahini (50 g)

3–4 medium-size parsnips (470 g)
(alternatively carrots)

6 teaspoons vinegar

2 tablespoons almond butter

2 teaspoons sesame oil

Iodized sea salt

1 avocado

1 carrot

1 scallion

2 nori sheets

Soy sauce, wasabi, and pickled ginger for serving

AH! "The wasabi paste that you find at organic grocery stores is not my favorite. My tip: buy organic horseradish in a jar (without cream) and then add a little matcha to give it the typical green color."

PREPARATION TIME: approx. 30 minutes

First cut tofu into slices and then into strips. Heat canola oil in a skillet and fry the tofu approx. 4–5 minutes. In the meantime, combine the soy sauce with 2 tablespoons agave syrup and tahini. Add this mixture to the skillet and allow to caramelize approx. 1 minute, until the tofu is crispy. Transfer to a plate lined with paper towels to drain.

For the parsnip rice, peel and coarsely grate the parsnips. Then chop with a knife so that the parsnip pieces are about the size of grains of rice. Mix the parsnips with the vinegar, almond butter, sesame oil, and ½ tablespoon agave syrup. Season lightly with salt.

Halve the avocado, remove the pit, spoon out the pulp with a spoon, and cut into strips. Peel the carrot and cut into fine strips. Clean and wash the scallion and cut in half lengthwise.

Place the nori sheets on a bamboo mat. Spread the parsnip rice out on the bottom third of the sheets and moisten the upper edge. Put half the tofu, avocado, scallion, and carrot on each and then roll up tightly. Cut the Maki Sushi rolls with a knife at an angle into bite-size pieces. Serve with soy sauce, wasabi paste, and ginger.

TOMATOCCINO
WITH ALMOND BASIL FOAM

INGREDIENTS for 4 glasses

Tomatoccino:

2 onions (150 g after onions are peeled)

1 small zucchini (150 g)

6 medium-size tomatoes (900 g)

3 tablespoons olive oil

1 teaspoon thyme leaves

½ chili pepper

1 level tablespoon chopped
rosemary leaves

5 sun-dried tomatoes in oil
(drained)

3 tablespoons white almond butter
(50 g)

1 level teaspoon iodized sea salt

Almond Basil Foam:

½ bunch of basil

4 tablespoons white almond butter
(60 g)

Grated peel of ¼ organic lemon

Iodized sea salt

Freshly ground black pepper

PREPARATION TIME: approx. 30 minutes

Peel the **onions** and coarsely chop. Wash the **zucchini** and **tomatoes** and coarsely chop. Heat **olive oil** in a saucepan. Sauté onions, **thyme**, zucchini, **chili pepper**, and **rosemary** in the oil for 3 minutes. Add both the fresh and **sun-dried tomatoes** and allow to cook approx. 7 minutes. In a blender, purée this mixture with the **almond butter**. Season with **salt**. If desired, water may be added.

Wash the **basil** and shake dry. Purée the basil leaves with almond butter, just over 1 cup (270 mL) water, and **lemon peel** in a blender. In a small saucepan, bring to a boil, **salt** and **pepper,** and then mix using an immersion blender or kitchen blender until frothy.

Put the tomato soup in glasses and top with Almond Basil Foam.

AH! "Tomatoes contain a large amount of lycopene, which is said to have a cancerpreventing effect. When heated, even more lycopene is released."

AVOCADO PAPRIKA EGGPLANT ROLLS WITH SUN-DRIED TOMATO SAUCE

INGREDIENTS for 2 people
(Approx. 8 rolls)

1 eggplant (220 g)

Approx. 3 tablespoons olive oil

Iodized sea salt

3 avocados (300 g pulp)

¼ chili pepper

1 organic lemon

Freshly ground black pepper

½ red bell pepper

½ yellow bell pepper

½ pint cherry tomatoes (150 g)

¼ cup sun-dried tomatoes in oil (30 g)

AH! "An easy and quick dish for summer. Eggplants are low in fat and rich in fiber. And avocados provide us with healthy unsaturated fatty acids and lots of vital substances. Eggplant Rolls also work great as appetizers."

PREPARATION TIME: approx. 30 minutes

Preheat oven to 480°F (250°C). Wash and pat eggplant dry. Cut off the ends and then cut the eggplant lengthwise into thin slices. Coat with 2 tablespoons olive oil and approx. ½ teaspoon salt. Place on a baking sheet lined with parchment paper and bake in the middle of the oven for approx. 10 minutes, until the eggplant slices take on a light color. Allow to cool for a short while. Cut the avocados in half and remove the pits. Spoon out the pulp with a spoon and place in a tall mixing container. Halve the chili pepper, remove the seeds and membranes, and finely chop. Wash the lemon with hot water, dry it off, and finely grate half of the peel. Squeeze 1 tablespoon juice from the lemon. Add the lemon peel, juice, and the chili pepper to the avocado and purée. Season with salt and pepper. Halve the bell peppers, remove the seeds, wash, and chop into fine pieces. Add to the avocado cream, and if desired, season with salt and pepper.

Wash the cherry tomatoes. Allow most of the liquid to drain from the sun-dried tomatoes. Purée both and then salt and pepper. Spread some of the avocado filling on each eggplant slice and then roll the slices up. To serve, place the rolls on the tomato sauce. Drizzle olive oil on top, as desired.

PUMPKIN AND BELL PEPPER VEGETABLE DISH WITH COCONUT TOFU STICKS

INGREDIENTS for 2 people

1 small Hokkaido pumpkin (800 g)

6 tablespoons olive oil

Iodized sea salt

1 red bell pepper

1 red onion

1 teaspoon curry powder

1⅔ cups coconut flakes (50 g)

½–1 chili pepper

1 scallion

6 ounces firm plain tofu (170 g)

2½ tablespoons peanut butter (40 g)

4 teaspoons soy sauce (20 mL)

1 tablespoon agave syrup

4 tablespoons coconut milk

AH! "Tofu contains a lot of protein and calcium and has been part of the Asian culinary tradition for a long time. I recommend a somewhat firmer tofu that has fewer air bubbles. The chili pepper gives this dish a little bit of a spicy kick and the capsaicin in the peppers stimulates fat burning in the body."

PREPARATION TIME: approx. 30 minutes

Preheat oven to 480°F (250°C). Wash the pumpkin and cut in half. Remove the seeds with a tablespoon and cut the pumpkin into cubes that are just under ½ inch (1 cm). Combine 2 tablespoons olive oil and ½ teaspoon salt. Coat the pumpkin with this mixture. Bake on the highest rung in the oven for approx. 15–18 minutes.

Cut the bell pepper in half, remove the seeds, wash, and chop into fine cubes. Peel and finely dice the onion. Heat 2 tablespoons olive oil in a skillet. Add curry powder and toast for a short amount of time. Add the onion and bell pepper and cook approx. 3 minutes over high heat. Mix with pumpkin and 2 tablespoons coconut flakes. Season with salt.

Wash the chili pepper and scallion and then cut both into rings. Cut the tofu into strips. Heat 2 tablespoons olive oil in a skillet and fry the tofu approx. 4 minutes. Combine the peanut butter, soy sauce, and agave syrup, and then add this mixture to the tofu and allow to caramelize approx. 1 minute. Add the coconut milk, stir, and then remove from heat. Dip all sides of the tofu into the remaining coconut flakes.

Place the pumpkin on plates. Arrange the tofu sticks on top and garnish with chili pepper and scallion rings.

RED TOWER
WITH AVOCADO CASHEW CREAM AND
CARAMELIZED TOFU

INGREDIENTS for 2 people

9 ounces red beets (260 g) (cooked, vacuum-sealed package)

10.5 ounces firm plain tofu (300 g)

3 tablespoons olive oil

2 teaspoons agave syrup

Iodized sea salt

Freshly ground black pepper

1 garlic clove

3 avocados

6½ tablespoons cashew butter (100 g)

1 tablespoon lemon juice

Some garden cress

Some walnut oil

PREPARATION TIME: approx. 20 minutes

Finely slice the red beets. Cut the tofu into slices that are about ¼ inch (5 mm) and then use a small glass to cut tofu circles that are the size of the red beets. Heat the olive oil in a skillet and fry the tofu approx. 3 minutes on each side. Add the agave syrup and a little salt, mix in evenly, and allow the tofu to caramelize approx. 20 seconds. Pepper and transfer to a plate lined with paper towels to drain for a short while.

Peel the garlic clove. Halve the avocados and remove the pits. Purée both with the cashew butter and lemon juice. Salt and pepper. Alternately layer the red beets, avocado cream, and tofu circles. Garnish with the garden cress and drizzle a little walnut oil on top.

AH! "Red beets are really a power vegetable. They contain large amounts of folic acid, iron, and calcium. On top of that, the red coloring agent betanin is one of the polyphenols, so it strengthens our immune system. Today, I buy red beets either fresh and cook them myself or I choose one of the vacuum-sealed varieties."

ROASTED VEGETABLES WITH TOFU CUBES AND ARTICHOKE YOGURT DIP

INGREDIENTS for 2 people

Roasted Vegetables:

3 carrots

2 zucchini

1 eggplant

1 fennel bulb

1 large head of broccoli (approx. 500 g)

Iodized sea salt

¼ of a small Hokkaido pumpkin (150 g)

6.5 ounces firm plain tofu (180 g)

8 tablespoons olive oil

1 teaspoon agave syrup

1 tablespoon chopped rosemary leaves

1 teaspoon dried oregano

Artichoke Yogurt Dip:

⅓ –½ cup artichoke hearts in oil (100 g)

½ bunch basil

1 cup soy yogurt (220 g)

Grated peel of ¼ organic lime

1 tablespoon lime juice

1 teaspoon agave syrup

Iodized sea salt

Freshly ground black pepper

PREPARATION TIME: approx. 35 minutes

Preheat oven to 480°F (250°C). Peel **carrots**, cut in half lengthwise, and slice into ½ inch (1 cm) rounds. Wash and slice **zucchini**. Wash and slice **eggplant** and **fennel bulb**. Wash **broccoli** and cut off 5⅓ cups (400 g) of florets. Cook the florets in well-salted boiling water for approx. 2 minutes, and then allow to drain in a sieve. Remove the seeds from the **pumpkin** and cut the pumpkin into pieces. Cut the **tofu** into cubes. Place everything in a large bowl and mix with **olive oil, agave syrup, herbs,** and approx. 1 teaspoon **sea salt.** Place on a baking sheet lined with parchment paper and bake on the highest rung in the oven for approx. 15–17 minutes, until the slices take on some color. Then put the vegetables on a plate lined with paper towels just long enough so that the excess oil can be absorbed.

In the meantime, you can prepare the dip. Allow the **artichokes** to drain and then finely chop. Wash the **basil,** shake dry, and finely chop the leaves. Mix the **soy yogurt** with the basil, artichokes, agave syrup, and some **lime peel** and **juice.** Season with **salt** and **pepper.**

BROCCOHOLIC
BROCCOLI WITH LEMON ALMOND CREAM

INGREDIENTS for 2 people

Iodized sea salt

1–2 heads of broccoli

1 organic lemon

½ cup white almond butter (120 g)

⅓ cup non-carbonated mineral water (80 mL)

Freshly ground black pepper

¼ cup whole almonds (40 g)

2 chili peppers

Olive oil to drizzle on top

AH! "This is a really quick dish to make. It's filling because you eat a lot of it and it's really healthy since it contains large amounts of cancer-preventing glucosinolate. It's also rich in Vitamin C, sodium, iron, zinc, and magnesium. To top it off, 1⅓ cups (100 g) of broccoli only has 24 calories. I like transforming typical side dishes into main dishes—and broccoli deserves to be a main dish as it is healthy, crisp, fresh, and delicious."

PREPARATION TIME: approx. 15 minutes

In a large saucepan, bring a little less than 2 inches (approx. 4 cm) of water to a boil. Season liberally with 1 teaspoon sea salt. Wash broccoli and cut 7½ cups (560 g) florets from the stalk. Add the florets to the well-salted boiling water and cook a total of approx. 3–4 minutes, stirring after 2 minutes. Then allow the broccoli to drain in a sieve. Wash the lemon in hot water and dry off. Finely grate half of the peel. Squeeze the juice from the lemon. Mix the juice and peel together with the almond butter and mineral water. Season with salt and pepper. Toast the almonds in a dry hot skillet approx. 3 minutes and then coarsely chop the almonds. Wash the chili peppers and cut into rings. Arrange the broccoli on a platter. Pour the Lemon Almond Cream on top. Garnish with chili peppers and chopped almonds. Drizzle some olive oil on top.

VEGETABLE LENTILS WITH SUNFLOWER LIME PESTO

INGREDIENTS for 2–3 people

Vegetable Lentils:

1⅓ cups brown lentils (250 g) (alternatively and quicker: cooked lentils in a can)

1 garlic clove

2 bay leaves

Iodized sea salt

3 tablespoons balsamic vinegar

3 tablespoons olive oil

1 zucchini

½ yellow bell pepper

1 onion

2 carrots

1 red beet (cooked, vacuum-sealed package)

Freshly ground black pepper

Sunflower Lime Pesto:

1 cup parsley leaves (40 g)

⅓ cup sunflower seeds (50 g)

4½ tablespoons olive oil (70 mL)

2 tablespoons lime juice

Grated peel of ¼ organic lime

½ teaspoon iodized sea salt

Freshly ground black pepper

PREPARATION TIME: approx. 60 minutes plus approx. 12 hours soaking time

Soak the **lentils** overnight in about 3 cups (750 mL) of water. Pour the lentils in a sieve, rinse, and allow to drain. Peel the **garlic clove** and then put through a garlic press. In a large saucepan, bring just over 4 cups (1 L) of water, lentils, **bay leaves,** garlic, and 1 teaspoon **salt** to a boil. Allow the lentils to cook approx. 40 minutes over high heat, until the water is absorbed. Remove from heat and mix in the **balsamic vinegar** and 1 tablespoon **olive oil.** In the meantime, you can prepare the pesto. Wash the **parsley,** shake dry, and pluck off the leaves. Purée together with the **sunflower seeds, olive oil, lime juice** and **peel,** and **salt** and **pepper.**

Wash the **zucchini.** Cut the **bell pepper** in half, remove the seeds, and wash. Cut both into small pieces. Peel and finely dice the **onion** and **carrots.** Cut the **red beet** into small cubes. Heat 2 tablespoons **olive oil** in a skillet and sauté the vegetables approx. 5 minutes over high heat. **Salt** and **pepper.** Carefully fold the vegetables into the lentils and season with **salt** and **pepper.** Serve the lentils on plates and top with the pesto.

MUSHROOM ALMOND LASAGNA WITH TOMATO CREAM

INGREDIENTS for 2 people

Mushroom Almond Lasagna:

About 22 mushrooms (500 g)

2 onions

2 garlic cloves

1 bunch thyme

5 tablespoons olive oil

²⁄₃ cup almonds (100 g)

2 tablespoons almond butter

Iodized sea salt

Freshly ground black pepper

4 zucchini

Tomato Cream:

1 onion

2 garlic cloves

2 tablespoons olive oil

4 sun-dried tomatoes in oil

1 teaspoon agave syrup

½ teaspoon oregano

6½ tablespoons tomato paste (100 g)

Iodized sea salt

Some basil for garnish

AH! "I always wash mushrooms and then let them dry on the window sill. It's the only way I can be sure that there isn't any dirt left on them. Every professional cook would object to this method, but that's just a strange habit of mine."

PREPARATION TIME: approx. 35 minutes

Clean mushrooms well, cut into slices, and then finely chop. Peel and finely chop onions and garlic cloves. Wash the thyme, shake dry, and remove the leaves. Heat 3 tablespoons olive oil in a skillet and sauté onions and garlic for 2 minutes. Add mushrooms and thyme and cook for an additional 7 minutes until the fluid is absorbed. Remove from heat.

Grind almonds in a blender. In a bowl, combine with the contents of the pan. Fold in the almond butter. Season liberally with salt and pepper.

Wash the zucchini. Using a vegetable slicer or a peeler, cut lengthwise into thin strips. For 2 servings of lasagna, you will need approx. 16 zucchini strips. Set the remaining zucchini aside to use later for the tomato cream. Then coat the zucchini with 2 tablespoons olive oil and 1 pinch of salt.

For the Tomato Cream, peel and finely chop the onion and garlic cloves. Chop the zucchini that was set to the side. Heat olive oil in a small saucepan. Sauté onion, garlic, and zucchini approx. 3 minutes. Allow most of the liquid to drain from the sun-dried tomatoes. Add the sun-dried tomatoes, tomato paste, agave syrup, and oregano to the skillet and allow everything to caramelize for 2 minutes. Add just under 7 tablespoons (100 mL) of water and finely purée in a blender. Salt. Place 2 slices of zucchini slightly on top of each other lengthwise on a plate. Spread some of the mushroom filling on top. For each piece of lasagna, use 4 layers of zucchini and then top with the Tomato Cream. If desired, use a really sharp knife to cut the lasagna into a rectangle shape. You might also like to garnish with basil before serving.

DELUXE WALNUT ENERGIZER
WITH "I LOVE SALAD" DRESSING

INGREDIENTS for 2 people

Deluxe Walnut Energizer:

9 ounces firm plain tofu (260 g)

4 tablespoons walnut oil

1 teaspoon gyros seasoning

1 teaspoon agave syrup

Iodized sea salt

3 cups lamb's lettuce or mixed baby greens (80 g)

1⅔ cups arugula (40 g)

1½ cups radicchio (40 g)

1 red beet (cooked, vacuum-sealed package)

1 zucchini

2 carrots

¾–1 cup corn (120 g)

1 level teaspoon curry powder

½ cup walnuts (60 g)

"I love Salad" Dressing:

⅔ cup sun-dried tomatoes in oil (80 g)

3 tablespoons olive oil (40 mL)

2 tablespoons chopped parsley

1 tablespoon lime juice

1 teaspoon agave syrup

2 teaspoons cashew butter

Iodized sea salt

Freshly ground black pepper

PREPARATION TIME: approx. 20 minutes

Cut tofu into cubes that are just under ½ inch (1 cm). Heat 3 tablespoons walnut oil in a skillet and fry the tofu for approx. 4 minutes over high heat. Stir in the gyros seasoning, agave syrup, and salt. Remove from heat, and if desired, season with salt again. Wash the salad greens and radicchio and spin dry. Cut the red beet into small cubes. Wash the zucchini and peel the carrots. Cut both into thin strips using a vegetable peeler. Allow the corn to drain. Heat 1 tablespoon walnut oil in a small skillet and sauté the corn with the curry powder 2–3 minutes. Salt. Toast the walnuts in a dry skillet for 2 minutes.

For the dressing, purée all ingredients except for the salt and pepper with just over 3 tablespoons (50 mL) water in a blender. Season with salt and pepper. In a bowl, mix the salad greens with the red beet cubes, corn, and carrot and zucchini strips. Fold in the dressing and serve with the tofu cubes and walnuts on top.

KOHLRABI RAVIOLI
WITH BELL PEPPER AND CASHEW FILLING
AND TOMATO BASIL SAUCE

INGREDIENTS for 2–3 people

2 kohlrabi

Iodized sea salt

Approx. 6 tablespoons olive oil

1 red bell pepper

1½ onions

¼ cup unsweetened cashew butter
(60 g)

2 pinches dried oregano

Freshly ground black pepper

2 tomatoes

½ bunch basil

2 garlic cloves

1 teaspoon agave syrup

AH! "Draining the kohlrabi on a plate lined with paper towels is really important because without this step the ravioli won't hold together later when they are stuffed. This is a light summer dish for which you will need a bit of finesse and a good slicer because the discs really do have to be paper thin. The somewhat more expensive gourmet or truffle slicers are perfect for the job."

PREPARATION TIME: approx. 30 minutes

Peel the kohlrabi and then use a slicer to cut into paperthin slices. Bring lightly salted water to a boil in a saucepan. Remove from heat and allow the kohlrabi to steam in the water for 10 minutes. Allow to drain first in a sieve and then approx. 2 minutes on a plate that is lined with paper towels. Combine 2 tablespoons olive oil and 1 pinch salt. Marinate the kohlrabi slices in this mixture.

For the filling, halve the bell pepper, remove the core, wash, and finely dice. Peel and finely chop the onions. Heat 1 tablespoon olive oil in a skillet. Sauté a third of the onions and bell pepper approx. 5 minutes over high heat, stirring occasionally. Transfer the mixture to a cutting board and then chop again with a knife so that the mixture is very fine. In a bowl, combine this mixture with the cashew butter and oregano. Season liberally with salt and pepper. Heat the mixture for a short time in a saucepan while stirring constantly—it should now have a creamy, thick consistency. Using a round cookie cutter, cut the Kohlrabi slices into discs. Put a teaspoon of the filling in the middle of each disc. Place a second kohlrabi circle on top and press down on the sides a little.

For the sauce, dice the tomatoes finely. Wash the basil, shake dry, and finely chop the leaves. Peel and finely chop the garlic cloves. Heat 2 tablespoons olive oil in a small skillet. Sauté the remaining onions and garlic approx. 2 minutes. Add the diced tomato and cook 2 minutes. Fold in the agave syrup and basil. Season with salt and pepper. Arrange the ravioli on a plate and drizzle tomato sauce and some olive oil on top. Garnish with basil leaves and stir.

ZUCCHINI SPAGHETTI VARIATIONS

A. **Basil Lime Pesto**

INGREDIENTS for 2 people

½– ⅔ cup pine nuts (80 g)

⅓ cup olive oil (80 mL)

Approx. 2 bunches basil (120 g)

2 tablespoons lime juice

1 tablespoon nutritional yeast
flakes (10 g)

1½ teaspoons iodized sea salt

Freshly ground black pepper

4 zucchini

PREPARATION TIME: approx. 10 minutes

Toast the **pine nuts** approx. 3 minutes in
4 teaspoons (20 mL) of **olive oil** in a skillet.
Wash the **basil**, spin dry, and coarsely
chop the leaves. Purée both together with
4 tablespoons (60 mL) of **olive oil**, **lime juice**,
nutritional yeast flakes, and **salt** and **pepper**.
If desired, **salt** and **pepper** again. Make
zucchini spaghetti using a spiral vegetable
cutter. Combine with the pesto and serve.

B. **Walnut Tomato Pesto**

INGREDIENTS for 2 people

¾–1 cup walnuts (100 g)

½ cup walnut oil (110 mL)

½ tablespoon nutritional yeast
flakes (5 g)

½ cup sun-dried tomatoes (50 g)

Freshly ground black pepper

4 zucchini

PREPARATION TIME: approx. 5 minutes

Toast the **walnuts** approx. 3 minutes in
4 teaspoons (20 mL) **walnut oil** in a skillet.
Purée all **ingredients** except for the zucchini.
Make zucchini spaghetti using a spiral
vegetable cutter. Combine with the pesto
and serve.

C. **Avocado Basil Cream**

INGREDIENTS for 2 people

4⅔ cups avocado pulp (700 g)

1 cup fresh basil (40 g)

2 tablespoons lemon juice

1 level teaspoon iodized sea salt

Freshly ground black pepper

4 pinches chili powder

4 zucchini

1 tablespoon olive oil

PREPARATION TIME: approx. 10 minutes

Cut **avocado pulp** into pieces. Wash **basil**, shake
dry, and chop coarsely. Using an immersion
blender or a kitchen blender, purée both together
with the **lemon juice**, **salt**, **pepper**, and **chili**
powder. If desired, **salt** and **pepper** again. Make
zucchini spaghetti using a spiral vegetable cutter
and combine with the avocado cream. Arrange
on plates and drizzle **olive oil** on top.

LAMB'S LETTUCE WITH AVOCADO PEAR DRESSING AND CARAMELIZED ALMONDS

INGREDIENTS for 2 people

Lamb's Lettuce Mixture:

1 red bell pepper

2 tablespoons olive oil

½ teaspoon agave syrup

1 pinch ground cinnamon

Iodized sea salt

2 cups radicchio (55 g)

6 cups lamb's lettuce or mixed
baby greens (190 g)

1 large carrot (130 g)

Almonds:

½ cup almonds (60 g)

2 pinches chili powder

2 pinches turmeric

1 tablespoon olive oil

1 tablespoon agave syrup

Iodized sea salt

Dressing:

1½ avocados

1 tablespoon white almond butter

4 tablespoons olive oil

¼ bunch parsley

Freshly ground black pepper

1 pear

Juice of 1 lemon

Iodized sea salt

PREPARATION TIME: approx. 15 minutes

Halve the bell pepper, remove the core, wash, and cut into fine strips. Heat the olive oil in a skillet and sauté the bell pepper approx. 3 minutes. Add the agave syrup and cinnamon and allow to caramelize for 30 seconds. Season with sea salt and transfer to a plate lined with paper towels to drain.

Cut the radicchio into fine strips. Wash both the radicchio and the lamb's lettuce or mixed baby greens and then spin dry. Peel the carrots and with a vegetable peeler, cut them into fine strips.

For the caramelized almonds, coarsely chop the almonds and toast with the chili powder and turmeric in olive oil in a skillet for 3 minutes. Add the agave syrup and a little salt and allow to caramelize approx. 20 seconds.

For the dressing, halve the avocados, and remove the core and 150 g pulp with a tablespoon. Finely chop the pulp, and mix with the almond butter and olive oil. Wash the parsley, shake dry, and finely chop. Peel and core the pear. Finely chop one half of the pear. Cut the other half into fine slices, drizzle some lemon juice on top, and set aside. Add the juice of ½ lemon, parsley, and chopped pear to the avocado. Season liberally with salt and pepper.

Mix the salad, carrots, and bell pepper with the dressing and arrange the pear slices on top. Sprinkle the caramelized almonds over the salad. If desired, drizzle olive oil on top.

SPINACH SAFFRON CREAM WITH ORANGE QUINOA

INGREDIENTS for 2 people

1½ cups quinoa (250 g)

Iodized sea salt

2 tablespoons olive oil

Grated peel of ½ organic

orange

13 cups spinach leaves (400 g)

1 onion

1 garlic clove

4½ tablespoons unsweetened

cashew butter (70 g)

2 pinches saffron threads

1 tablespoon walnut oil

3 tablespoons cashews (30 g)

AH! "Wash the spinach really well. Otherwise, you'll end up grinding dirt between your teeth. For an even more delicate, sweet taste, I recommend using baby spinach when it is in season and available."

PREPARATION TIME: approx. 30 minutes

Rinse the quinoa in a sieve for a short while and then cook in a little over 3 cups (750 mL) of lightly salted boiling water approx. 17 minutes uncovered over high heat until the water has been absorbed. Stir occasionally. Combine the olive oil and orange peel with the quinoa. Salt, as desired.

In the meantime, wash the spinach thoroughly, remove the thick stems, and cut into large pieces. Peel and finely chop the onion and garlic clove. Purée cashew butter with just over ¾ cup (200 mL) water and the saffron threads in a blender. Heat the walnut oil in a skillet. Sauté the onion and garlic approx. 3 minutes. Add the spinach and cook approx. 2 minutes. Add the Cashew Saffron Cream and cook approx. 1 minute until the mixture has thickened. Season with salt. Toast the cashews in a dry skillet approx. 3 minutes.

Use an ice cream scoop to make quinoa scoops and place both the quinoa and spinach on plates. Sprinkle cashews on top before serving.

ZUCCHINI LASAGNA WITH BOLOGNESE LAYERS AND ALMOND CREAM

INGREDIENTS for 1 person

6.5 ounces firm plain tofu (180 g)

1 onion

1 garlic clove

1 large carrot (120 g)

Approx. 4 tablespoons olive oil

½ cup tomato paste (130 g)

1 teaspoon oregano

1½ teaspoons agave syrup

4½ tablespoons red wine (70 mL)

Iodized sea salt

Freshly ground black pepper

½ bunch basil

1 tablespoon white almond butter (15 g)

2 teaspoons non-carbonated mineral water (10 mL)

1 zucchini

A few basil leaves for garnish

AH! "This lasagna is really close to traditional lasagna made with white flour. But it provides you with a lot of vital substances, lots of vitamins, high-quality protein, and Mediteranean spices. I'm a pasta fan, and for me this dish is unbeatable. Garfield himself would be excited about this dish."

PREPARATION TIME: approx. 25 minutes

Preheat oven to 480°F (250°C).

Mash tofu with a fork. Peel and finely chop onion, garlic clove, and carrots. Heat 2 tablespoons olive oil in a skillet and fry the tofu approx. 3 minutes. Add the vegetables and sauté 3 minutes while stirring. Fold in the tomato paste, oregano, and agave syrup, and cook 1 minute longer. Pour in the red wine and allow to cook for 30 seconds. Season with salt and pepper. Remove from heat. Wash the basil and shake dry. Finely chop the leaves and fold into the filling. Combine the almond butter and mineral water. Salt and pepper.

Using a vegetable slicer or a peeler, cut the zucchini into paper-thin slices. Coat with 1 tablespoon olive oil and 1 pinch sea salt. Place 2 slices of zucchini slightly on top of each other on a plate. Spread 2 tablespoons of the Bolognese filling on top. Continue to layer zucchini slices and filling until there are no more ingredients. When you are finished, pour the almond cream evenly over the top. Put the lasagna back into the oven for about 5 more minutes at 480°F (250°C). If desired, drizzle olive oil over the top and garnish with basil leaves.

ZUCCHINILONI WITH PUMPKIN OLIVE FILLING AND BASIL PESTO

INGREDIENTS for 2 people

½ medium-size Hokkaido pumpkin (580 g)

6 tablespoons olive oil

Iodized sea salt

1 onion

8 black olives (not pitted)

½ chili pepper

1 teaspoon chopped parsley

Freshly ground black pepper

2 zucchini

1 small bunch basil (40 g)

1 tablespoon lemon juice

1 tablespoon pistachios (10 g)

AH! "This dish is incredibly delicious and light, and it's a feast for the eyes. For perfect results, you will need a slicer since that's the best way to cut the zucchini paper thin. After a couple of tries, you should be able to get your rolls to look quite nice."

PREPARATION TIME: approx. 30 minutes

Preheat the oven to 480°F (250°C).

Wash and halve the pumpkin. Remove the seeds. Cut about one-third (450 g) of the pumpkin into thin slices. Toss with 2 tablespoons olive oil and about ½ teaspoon salt. Place on a baking sheet lined with parchment paper and bake on the highest rung in the oven approx. 15 minutes, until the pumpkin takes on a little color. Then allow to cool for a short while.

In the meantime, peel and finely chop the onion. Remove the olive pits with a knife and then finely chop the olives. Remove the seeds and membranes from the chili pepper. Next, wash and finely chop the chili pepper. Wash the parsley, shake dry, and finely chop the leaves. Chop the pumpkin into medium-size pieces. Heat 1 tablespoon olive oil in a skillet. Sauté the onion, chili pepper, and olives approx. 3 minutes. Fold in pumpkin and parsley. Season with salt and pepper. Wash zucchini and cut lengthwise into paper-thin slices with a vegetable slicer. For 4 rolls, you will need approx. 24 zucchini slices. Coat with 1 tablespoon olive oil and a little sea salt. Place 6 slices of zucchini in a row slightly on top of each other. Spread the pumpkin filling from top to bottom and roll up carefully as you would if you were rolling sushi. Bake the Zucchiniloni approx. 5 minutes in the oven. Wash basil, shake dry, and pluck off the leaves. Purée with lemon juice and 2 tablespoons olive oil. Salt and pepper. Shell the pistachios and coarsely chop them.

Arrange the Zucchiniloni on plates and garnish with pesto and chopped pistachios. Serve.

ZUCCHINI RIBBON NOODLES
WITH SPINACH ALMOND SAUCE

INGREDIENTS for 1 person

3⅓ cups baby spinach (100 g)

3 tablespoons white almond butter (50 g)

6½ tablespoons non-carbonated mineral water (100 mL)

1 red onion

1 garlic clove

4 sun-dried tomatoes in oil

2 tablespoons roasted hazelnuts (15 g)

4 zucchini

3 tablespoons olive oil

1 pinch turmeric

Iodized sea salt

Freshly ground black pepper

PREPARATION TIME: approx. 20 minutes

Wash the baby spinach and spin dry. Combine the almond butter and mineral water. Peel and finely chop the onion and garlic clove. Allow the sun-dried tomatoes to drain and then finely chop. Coarsely chop the hazelnuts. Wash the zucchini and using a peeler, peel long strips that resemble ribbon noodles. Rotate the zucchini as you are peeling until only the soft inside with the seeds remains. Heat 2 tablespoons olive oil in a skillet. Sauté the onions and turmeric for 2 minutes. Add the garlic and sun-dried tomatoes. Sauté an additional 2 minutes. Add the almond butter and baby spinach and allow to cook 1–2 minutes while stirring. Liberally season with salt and pepper. Remove from heat. Toss zucchini with a mixture of 1 tablespoon olive oil and 1 pinch sea salt, and then add to the Spinach Almond Cream and heat for 30 seconds. Sprinkle hazelnuts on top before serving.

AH! "It works well to use the remaining zucchini for a soup or sauce."

LOW-CARB PIZZA

INGREDIENTS for 2 people

Pizza Dough:

3½ tablespoons whole flax seeds (50 g)

1⅓ cups blanched almonds (200 g)

1 small to medium-size zucchini (180 g)

1 teaspoon dried oregano

2 tablespoons olive oil

1 teaspoon iodized sea salt

Cheese Sauce:

2½ tablespoons white almond butter (40 g)

1 teaspoon nutritional yeast flakes

2 pinches turmeric

4 teaspoons non-carbonated mineral water (20 mL)

Iodized sea salt

Topping:

2 tomatoes

¾ cup mushrooms (70 g)

1 onion

1 garlic clove

½ eggplant

½ zucchini

1 orange bell pepper

3 tablespoons olive oil

⅓ cup tomato paste (80 g)

1 teaspoon oregano

4 teaspoons non-carbonated mineral water (20 mL)

½ teaspoon iodized sea salt

PREPARATION TIME: approx. 35 minutes plus approx. 80 minutes drying time in the oven or approx. 12 hours drying time in a dehydrator

For the pizza dough, grind the flax seeds and almonds in a blender until they have the consistency of flour. Add the zucchini, oregano, olive oil, and sea salt and purée everything to a fine mixture. Split the dough in half. Place each of the halves between two sheets of plastic wrap and roll out with a rolling pin. Allow to dry in a dehydrator at 155°F (68°C) for approx. 12 hours or in the oven on a baking sheet lined with parchment paper at 250°F (120°C) for approx. 80 minutes or a bit longer for a crisper crust.

For the cheese sauce, stir all ingredients until you have a smooth mixture. If desired, salt again.

For the topping, wash the tomatoes and cut into very thin slices. Wash the mushrooms and cut into thin slices. Peel the onion and garlic clove. Cut the onion into thin rings and finely chop the garlic. Wash the eggplant and zucchini. Cut the eggplant into small cubes. Cut the zucchini into strips with a vegetable peeler. Halve the bell pepper, remove the core, wash, and cut into thin strips. Heat 3 tablespoons olive oil in a skillet. Add all of the vegetables except for the tomatoes and zucchini and sauté approx. 5–7 minutes. Combine the tomato paste, oregano, and mineral water to make a sauce and then salt. Spread the tomato sauce on the two pizza crusts. Top first with the tomato slices, then with the sautéed vegetables, and finally with the zucchini strips. Pour the cheese sauce on top and if desired, drizzle olive oil over everything. Bake in the oven at 480°F (250° C) for approx. 5–7 minutes.

AH! "When you are making the pizza, make sure to roll the dough out thin. This is the only way to get a crispy crust. Flax seeds contain a lot of fiber, which helps you to stay full for a long time. I can hardly taste a difference between this pizza and "real" pizza. The taste of the creamy cheese that you get from the almonds can't be beat. I really don't miss cheese made from cow's milk anymore."

WHITE BEANS IN BASIL TOMATO SAUCE

INGREDIENTS for 2 people

1 tablespoon sunflower seeds

2 ounces smoked tofu (50 g)

1 red onion

4 cups cooked white beans (250 g) (can)

1–2 tablespoons olive oil

2 pinches turmeric

⅓ cup tomato paste (80 g)

6 tablespoons non-carbonated
mineral water (90 mL)

1 teaspoon agave syrup

1 bunch basil

1 carrot

Iodized sea salt

Freshly ground black pepper

PREPARATION TIME: approx. 20 minutes

Toast the **sunflower seeds** approx. 2 minutes in a dry skillet and then place in a small bowl. Cut **smoked tofu** into small cubes. Peel and finely chop the **onion**. Allow the **beans** to drain. Heat 1 tablespoon **olive oil** in a skillet and fry the tofu approx. 3 minutes.

Add the **turmeric** and onions and cook approx. 2 minutes. Then add the beans, **tomato paste**, **mineral water**, and **agave syrup** and cook 2 minutes. Remove from heat and season the beans with **salt** and **pepper**.

Wash the **basil**, shake dry, and finely chop the leaves. Peel the **carrot** and cut into fine strips using a vegetable peeler. Place the beans on plates. Garnish with the basil, carrot strips, and sunflower seeds. Drizzle some **olive oil** on top.

AH! "Amazingly simple, but oh so delicious. The simplest things are often the best. My publisher—by the way, the best publisher in the world—also completed the Challenge, and he ate this dish for breakfast. I couldn't do that, but people's tastes are just different. Beans contain a lot of protein."

GREEN WARRIOR

INGREDIENTS for 2 people

2 heads of broccoli

2 cups sugar snap peas (200 g)

½ bunch green asparagus (250 g)

1⅔ cups frozen peas (200 g)

Iodized sea salt

2 zucchini

2 tablespoons olive oil

½ bunch basil

½ bunch parsley

4 tablespoons white almond butter (60 g)

2½ tablespoons cashew butter (40 g)

⅔ cup non-carbonated mineral water (160 mL)

Grated peel of ½ organic lemon

Freshly ground black pepper

4 scallions

OPTIONAL: Yogurt Dressing

½ bunch basil

½ bunch parsley

Some lemon juice

Grated peel of ½ organic lemon

2¼ cups soy yogurt (500 g)

2 tablespoons olive oil

Iodized sea salt

Freshly ground black pepper

PREPARATION TIME: approx. 20 minutes

Wash the broccoli and cut off approx. 8 cups (600 g) of broccoli florets from the stalk. Wash the sugar snap peas, allow to dry, and cut in half at an angle. Wash the asparagus, peel the skin off the bottom third, and cut off the ends. Then cut the asparagus into bite-size pieces. Cook the peas in lightly salted, boiling water in a large saucepan for 3 minutes. Add the broccoli florets, asparagus, and sugar snap peas and cook for 2–3 minutes, until the vegetables are al dente. Allow to drain in a sieve. Wash the zucchini and peel into strips with a vegetable peeler. Marinate the vegetables in the olive oil.

Wash the herbs, shake dry, and coarsely chop the leaves. Combine the almond and cashew butter with the mineral water, lemon peel, and herbs in a blender. Heat in a small saucepan so that the sauce gets a little thicker. Season with salt and pepper.

Clean, wash, and finely chop the scallions. Arrange the vegetables and top with the sauce and scallions. For the yogurt sauce, wash the herbs, shake dry, and coarsely chop the leaves. Purée with the remaining ingredients in a blender. Season with salt and pepper.

ZUCCHINI RIBBON NOODLES WITH RED BELL PEPPER TOMATO SAUCE AND WALNUT CRUMBLE

INGREDIENTS for 2 people

2 red bell peppers

2 red onions

6 sun-dried tomatoes in oil

⅓ cup walnuts (40 g)

Iodized sea salt

Approx. 5 tablespoons olive oil

4 tablespoons tomato paste

½ teaspoon agave syrup

2 teaspoons dried oregano

Freshly ground black pepper

2 zucchini

AH! "This is one of the fast dishes that is good for both stressful days and for when you need a big shot of vitamins. For optimal results, you will need a good peeler. Walnuts contain a lot of linoleic acid, an Omega-3 fatty acid that is good for your heart, and since 100 g of walnuts contain 7,490 mg of this fatty acid, they are the king of nuts."

PREPARATION TIME: approx. 15 minutes

Halve the red bell peppers, remove the core, wash well, and then cut into small cubes. Peel and finely chop the onions. Allow most of the liquid to drain from the sun-dried tomatoes and then finely chop. Toast walnuts in a dry pan approx. 2 minutes. Then coarsely purée in a blender with a little sea salt.

Heat 4 tablespoons olive oil in a skillet and then sauté onions and bell peppers approx. 3–4 minutes. Add tomato paste, sun-dried tomatoes, agave syrup, and oregano and cook for 30 seconds while stirring. Salt and pepper. Wash zucchini, and using a vegetable peeler, peel long strips that resemble ribbon noodles. Rotate the zucchini as you are peeling until only the soft inside with the seeds remains. Add the zucchini strips to the skillet and mix with the sauce. Arrange on plates and sprinkle Walnut Crumble on top. If desired, drizzle with olive oil.

QUINOA LENTIL CUPS WITH SAFFRON AND RED CABBAGE

INGREDIENTS for 2–3 people

Quinoa Lentil Boats:

1¼ cups quinoa (200 g)

2⅓ cups non-carbonated mineral water (550 mL)

Iodized sea salt

2 cups red cabbage (200 g)

2 tablespoons canola oil

1¾ cups cooked green lentils (130 g)

2 pinches ground saffron

Freshly ground black pepper

A few leaves from 1 small white cabbage

1–2 chili peppers for garnish

Dip:

½ cup soy yogurt (120 g)

1 tablespoon lime juice

Iodized sea salt

2½ tablespoons dark almond butter (40 g)

PREPARATION TIME: approx. 30 minutes

Rinse quinoa in a fine sieve for a short while. Place quinoa, 2¼ cups (550 mL) mineral water, and approx. ½ teaspoon salt in a small saucepan. Cook uncovered over high heat approx. 17 minutes, until the water is completely absorbed. Wash and clean the red cabbage and then cut into fine strips. Heat canola oil in a skillet and sauté red cabbage for 3–4 minutes. Add the quinoa and cook for 3 more minutes. Add the lentils and then season with the saffron, sea salt, and pepper. Remove several leaves from the head of white cabbage and fill these with the Quinoa Lentils.

Clean the chili peppers and cut into rings. For the dip, add the lime juice and sea salt to the soy yogurt to taste. Then carefully stir in the almond butter with a fork so that the dip has a marble appearance. Top the boats with the dip and the chili peppers.

AH! "When buying soy yogurt, make sure that it isn't sweetened. There are now brands of soy yogurt that contain sugar even though they are labeled as natural."

ALMOND PEA SOUP
WITH WALNUT MINT PESTO

INGREDIENTS for 2 people

Soup:

2 onions

3 tablespoons olive oil

⅔ cups non-carbonated mineral water (630 mL)

2⅓ cups frozen peas (300 g)

¼ cup white almond butter (60 g)

Iodized sea salt

Freshly ground black pepper

1 red chilli pepper for garnish

Some mint for garnish

Some walnut oil for garnish

Pesto:

1 small bunch flat-leaf parsley (40 g)

½ cup mint leaves (10 g)

1 cup walnuts (120 g)

6½ tablespoons walnut oil (100 mL)

2 tablespoons lemon juice

1 level teaspoon iodized sea salt

Freshly ground black pepper

PREPARATION TIME: approx. 25 minutes

Peel the **onions** and coarsely chop. Heat the **olive oil** in a saucepan and sauté onions for 3 minutes. Add **mineral water** and **peas** and allow to cook in a covered saucepan approx. 12 minutes (sticks easily). Then purée until smooth and fold in the **almond butter**. If you like, add a little more water and season with **pepper** and 1 level teaspoon **salt**.

For the pesto, wash the **parsley** and **mint** and shake both dry. Pluck the parsley leaves off. Toast **walnuts** in a dry pan approx. 3 minutes. Purée these with all other **ingredients** for the pesto in a blender. Serve the soup in wide shallow bowls with pesto on top. If desired, arrange the chili pepper rings and **mint** on the soup and drizzle several drops of **walnut oil** on top before serving.

AH! "I always buy fresh mint as a bunch and not in a pot because I've noticed a difference in taste, and the bunched mint simply tastes better to me. Walnuts provide us with the necessary Omega-3 fatty acids and peas are truly a powerhouse vegetable as they contain large amounts of protein, vitamins, minerals, and fiber that keep us full for a long time."

MIXED FORCES PLATE

INGREDIENTS for 2 people

Mixed Forces Plate:

1 very small Hokkaido pumpkin (600 g)

1 teaspoon paprika

Iodized sea salt

Approx. 7 tablespoons olive oil

1 garlic clove

½–1 eggplant (190 g)

1–2 heads of broccoli

1 tablespoon lemon juice

Herb salt

3½ tablespoons sunflower seeds (30 g)

Hummus:

1¼ cups cooked chickpeas (200 g)

2 tablespoons dark tahini (30 g)

1 tablespoon lemon juice

½ teaspoon ground cumin

½ teaspoon iodized sea salt

3 tablespoons cold, non-carbonated mineral water (40 mL)

In addition:

1 chili pepper

¼ bunch flat-leaf parsley

Paprika

PREPARATION TIME: approx. 30 minutes

Preheat oven to 480°F (250°C).

Wash the pumpkin, cut it in half, and scoop out the seeds. Use a sharp knife to cut the pumpkin into wedges. Toss with paprika, sea salt, and 2 tablespoons olive oil. For the eggplant, peel and finely chop the garlic clove. Wash the eggplant and cut into slices. To season, toss with 2 tablespoons olive oil, garlic, and sea salt. Spread the pumpkin and eggplant out evenly on a baking sheet lined with parchment paper. Bake on the highest rung in the oven approx. 15–17 minutes.

Wash the broccoli and cut off approx. 6½ cups (500 g) of broccoli florets from the stalk. Cook in well-salted boiling water approx. 3 minutes. Allow to drain in a sieve. Gently toss with 2 tablespoons olive oil, lemon juice, herb salt, and sunflower seeds.

For the hummus, purée all ingredients in a blender. Wash the chili pepper and cut into fine rings. Wash the parsley, shake dry, and finely chop.

Divide the hummus in half and place each half in the middle of a plate. Sprinkle paprika and chopped parsley on top and drizzle with a liberal amount of olive oil. Arrange the pumpkin, broccoli, and eggplant around the hummus. Garnish the eggplant with the chili pepper rings and some parsley.

RED LENTIL SOUP

INGREDIENTS for 2 people

1 white onion (approx. 115 g)

1 garlic clove

1 carrot (approx. 110 g)

3 tablespoons olive oil

¾ cup red lentils (150 g)

4 sun-dried tomatoes in oil
(drained)

1 tablespoon white almond butter

1 teaspoon agave syrup

2 tablespoons lemon juice

1 teaspoon iodized sea salt

Freshly ground black pepper

¼ bunch basil

¼ bunch oregano

½ chili pepper

⅓ cup hazelnuts (40 g)

2 tablespoons hazelnut oil

PREPARATION TIME: approx. 20 minutes

Peel and coarsely chop the onion and garlic clove. Peel the carrot and cut into medium-size pieces. Heat olive oil in a medium saucepan. Sauté the onion, garlic, and carrot approx. 3 minutes. Add lentils and 3¾ cups (900 mL) water; cook in a covered saucepan over high heat approx. 8 minutes. Then purée with 1 sun-dried tomato, almond butter, and agave syrup. Add a little more water, if needed. Add 1 tablespoon lemon juice and season with salt and pepper.

Wash the herbs, shake dry, and finely chop. Remove the seeds and membranes from the chili pepper, wash, and finely chop. Toast the hazelnuts in a dry skillet for 3 minutes and then coarsely chop. Finely chop the remaining sun-dried tomatoes. Toss these prepared ingredients in a bowl with the hazelnut oil and 1 tablespoon lemon juice. Salt and pepper. Put the soup in bowls and top with the Herb Nut Mixture.

AH! "Lentils are very rich in protein, and they contain a lot of zinc and iron. You don't have to soak red lentils like you do brown lentils. So, this is a dish that can be put together really quickly."

ASIAN SESAME BURGER

INGREDIENTS for 2 people

Asian Slaw:

2 cups Chinese cabbage (220 g)

1 carrot

½ chili pepper

½ bunch flat-leaf parsley

¼ cup tomato paste (60 g)

2 tablespoons peanut oil

1 tablespoon soy sauce

1 tablespoon agave syrup

3 tablespoons cashew butter (50 g)

1 tablespoon white wine vinegar

1 tablespoon fresh ginger,
chopped

Iodized sea salt

Breaded Tofu:

⅔ cup whole wheat flour (70 g)

6 tablespoons non-carbonated
mineral water (90 mL)

½ teaspoon iodized sea salt

½ cup light sesame seeds (50 g)

⅓ cup dark sesame seeds (30 g)

7 ounces firm plain tofu (200 g)

5 tablespoons canola oil

In addition:

1 red bell pepper

1 tablespoon sesame oil

Soy sauce

¼ cucumber

2 Vegan for Fit Burger Buns
(For recipe, see page 104)

PREPARATION TIME: approx. 30 minutes

Wash and clean the Chinese cabbage and then cut into fine strips. Peel and coarsely grate the carrot. Remove the seeds and membranes from the chili pepper. Wash and finely chop the chili pepper. Wash the parsley, shake dry, and finely chop the leaves. Mix the parsley with the chili pepper and the other ingredients for the Asian Slaw and stir until the sauce is creamy. Season with salt and then mix with the Chinese cabbage and carrot.

For the breaded tofu, whisk the flour, mineral water, and salt until creamy and pour into a shallow bowl. Mix the light and dark sesame seeds together and pour into a second shallow bowl. Cut the tofu into thin slices. Heat the canola oil in a skillet. Dip the tofu into the flour mixture and dredge in the sesame seeds. Fry approx. 3–4 minutes on each side over medium heat. Then transfer to a plate lined with paper towels to drain.

Halve the bell pepper, remove the core, wash, and cut into fine strips. Sauté in hot sesame oil for 3 minutes; season with some soy sauce. Wash the cucumber and cut into fine strips. Cut the burger buns in half. Spread the Asian Slaw on the bottom halves. Then add the sesame tofu, bell pepper, and cucumber. Put the other half of the bun on top.

QUINOA CROQUETTES

INGREDIENTS for approx.
10 croquettes

Quinoa Croquettes:

1¼ cups quinoa (200 g)

2⅓ cups non-carbonated mineral
water (550 mL)

Iodized sea salt

2 medium-size red onions

1 bunch parsley

2 rounded teaspoons mustard

2 rounded teaspoons locust bean
gum (If not available, you can use guar gum.)

1 teaspoon sweet paprika

Freshly ground black pepper

3–4 tablespoons olive oil

Tomato Dip:

1 medium-size tomato (100 g)

¾ cup soy yogurt (170 g)

3 sun-dried tomatoes (drained)

1 teaspoon agave syrup

Iodized sea salt

Freshly ground black pepper

PREPARATION TIME: approx. 40 minutes

In a fine sieve, rinse the quinoa off with water.
In a small saucepan, cook the quinoa with
mineral water and approx. ½ teaspoon sea salt
over high heat approx. 17 minutes, until the
water is absorbed.

In the meantime, peel and finely chop the
onions. Wash the parsley, shake dry, and finely
chop the leaves.

Mix the quinoa together with the mustard,
locust bean gum, paprika, parsley, and onions,
and then knead together. The mixture should
hold together. Season liberally with salt and
pepper. If the quinoa mixture is a bit too dry,
add a little more water. Shape into croquettes
and fry in hot olive oil over medium to high heat
approx. 4 minutes on each side. The croquettes
should take on a little color. Transfer to a plate
lined with paper towels to drain.

For the dip, mix all ingredients in a blender.
If desired, season again with salt and pepper.

AH! "Cook the quinoa the day before so that you
can prepare these croquettes even quicker. It's
important to add the right amount of water to the
croquette mixture; the best thing to do is to knead
the mixture thoroughly with your hands, and then
you'll be able to feel whether or not it is going to
hold together well. Kneading is important because
it activates the locust bean gum."

ASPARAGUS ORANGE SOUP

INGREDIENTS for 2 people

½ bunch white asparagus (260 g)

1 white onion

2 tablespoons walnut oil

6½ tablespoons orange juice (100 mL)

Grated peel of ½ organic orange

2½ tablespoons white almond

butter (40 g)

Iodized sea salt

4 or 5 green asparagus tips (100 g)

A little organic lemon zest

PREPARATION TIME: approx. 20 minutes

Wash and peel the white asparagus and cut off the woody ends. Cut the asparagus into medium-size pieces. Peel and finely chop the onion. Heat 1 tablespoon walnut oil in a small saucepan and sauté the onion for 2 minutes. Add the asparagus and sauté for an additional 2 minutes. Deglaze with 1⅔ cups (400 mL) water and cook covered over high heat approx. 10 minutes.

Purée the asparagus, asparagus cooking water, and onions with the orange juice, orange peel, and almond butter in a powerful blender until smooth. Then using a whisk (this makes it quicker), press the mixture through a fine sieve so that the soup is smooth and the bitter pieces are removed. Season with salt.

Wash the asparagus tips and sauté in 1 tablespoon hot walnut oil in a skillet approx. 3 minutes. Garnish the soup with the asparagus tips and a little lemon zest.

AH! "Asparagus only has 17 calories per 100 g—a great vegetable for losing weight quickly. You can make this soup really quickly, but pressing it through a sieve is essential. If you skip this step, the soup will taste bitter."

ZUCCHINI WITH AMARANTH FILLING

INGREDIENTS for 2 people

½ cup amaranth (100 g) (not popped)

2–2¼ cups non-carbonated
mineral water (510 mL)

Iodized sea salt

1 red onion

1 garlic clove

2 ounces smoked tofu (60 g)

3 tablespoons olive oil

¼ cup tomato paste (60 g)

½ teaspoon agave syrup

2 tablespoons white almond butter
(30 g)

2 teaspoons lemon juice

2 zucchini

A few oregano and thyme stems
for garnish

PREPARATION TIME: approx. 45 minutes

In a saucepan, bring the amaranth with a little more than
2 cups (500 mL) mineral water and 1 pinch sea salt just
to a boil. Allow to cook covered over low to medium heat
approx. 20–25 minutes, stirring occasionally.

Peel and finely chop the onion and garlic clove. Cut the
smoked tofu into small cubes. Heat 1 tablespoon olive oil
in a skillet and fry the tofu approx. 3 minutes. Add the onion
and garlic and cook 2 more minutes. Stir in the tomato
paste, amaranth, and agave syrup. Season liberally with
salt and pepper.

Preheat the oven to 480°F (250°C).

Combine the almond butter, lemon juice, and 2 teaspoons
(10 mL) mineral water. Season liberally with salt.

Cut the zucchini in half lengthwise with a sharp knife and
carefully scoop out the inside with a teaspoon. Combine
2 tablespoons olive oil and a little sea salt and coat the
zucchini with this mixture. Spoon the amaranth filling
into the zucchinis and top with the almond cream. Bake
in the middle of the oven approx. 9 minutes. Garnish
with oregano and thyme stems, as desired.

AH! "White almond butter mixed with
some water and spices works really
well for au gratin dishes. However,
you've got to wait for just the right
moment. The sauce should be golden
brown, but not yet crumbly."

BETWEEN MEALS

Healthy and delicious snacks for when you all of a sudden get hungry are no longer just wishful thinking. You can prepare them at home and then put them together at work or elsewhere with just a few quick steps. If you lead an active lifestyle, then high quality snacks are just the thing for you. Then you can avoid feeling weak and instead have energy for everything you do during the day, without having to rely on the often pitiful offerings from snack bars, convenience stores, and the like. A few amaranth bars and some organic fruit in your bag along with a quinoa salad and your day can begin.

SNACKS

RECIPES

CHILI CRACKERS

INGREDIENTS for 15 crackers

1 cup sunflower seeds (130 g)

2⅓ cups flax seeds (250 g)

1 level teaspoon iodized sea salt

6½ tablespoons tomato paste (100 g)

1 level teaspoon chili powder
(to taste)

2 pinches turmeric

PREPARATION TIME: approx. 10 minutes plus approx. 45 minutes drying time in the oven or 6½ hours of drying time in the dehydrator

Grind **sunflower seeds** to a powder in a blender. Mix with the other **ingredients** in a large bowl and roll out on a dehydrator baking tray lined with a dehydrator non-stick sheet into a 11¼ x 8¼ inches (29 x 22 cm) rectangle. Alternatively, you can roll out the dough between 2 sheets of parchment paper on a baking sheet. To do this, put the dough on a sheet of parchment paper, flatten slightly using your hands, cover with a second piece of parchment paper, and roll the dough out with a rolling pin until you have a smooth, flat rectangle. If the rectangle isn't even on the edges, then mold it back together with your hands into the proper shape and roll over again with the rolling pin. Allow the crackers to dry in the dehydrator at 155°F (68°C) for approx. 6½ hours or in the oven at 175°F (80°C) for approx. 45 minutes. Then cut the crackers into a diamond shape with a sharp knife.

AH! "This is a low-carb alternative to crispbread or crackers. You can make them very quickly, they're very filling, and they're high in fiber. I often make a few trays of crackers and snack on them through the week with salads or with homemade spreads."

BEST SNACK BARS IN THE WORLD
AMARANTH BARS WITH CHERRIES AND ALMONDS

INGREDIENTS for approx.

20 bars

11 ounces cocoa butter (320 g)

6 cups popped amaranth (240 g)

2 level teaspoons ground vanilla

⅔ cup chopped, roasted almonds (80 g)

1 cup dried cherries (160 g)

1 cup agave syrup (240 g)

¾ cup white almond butter (200 g)

⅓ cup organic cocoa (40 g)

2 teaspoons ground cinnamon

1 pinch iodized sea salt

PREPARATION TIME: approx. 25 minutes plus approx. 30–60 minutes cooling time

Melt the cocoa butter in a small saucepan over a hot water bath. Mix together the melted cocoa butter with the other ingredients. Place the mixture on parchment paper and mold it into a rectangle about 14 x 8 inches (36 x 20 cm) and with a thickness of a little more than a half an inch (1.5 cm). Place a second piece of parchment paper on top and gently press down with your hands until you have a smooth surface. Place the bars in the freezer for 30 minutes or in the refrigerator for 60 minutes. Then cut into approx. 20 bars with a sharp knife.

AH! "These bars are made with high quality ingredients and are perfect for when you are on the go. Just prepare the bars on the weekend; then you'll have enough to snack on for the week. Good cocoa butter—it's best if you can buy a raw food version—is easiest to find online. Just search for 'organic' and 'cocoa butter': it's also cheaper online!"

TORTILLA CHIPS WITH AVOCADOS AND CASHEW CHEESE

INGREDIENTS for 1–2 people

2 avocados

1 tablespoon lemon juice

Iodized sea salt

Freshly ground black pepper

3 tablespoons cashew butter (50 g)

2 tablespoons non-carbonated mineral water (30 mL)

1 teaspoon nutritional yeast flakes

¼ red bell pepper

¼ yellow bell pepper

1 chili pepper

1 scallion

1 cup blue tortilla chips (35 g)
(made from 100% corn)

1 cup BBQ tortilla chips (35 g)
(made from 100% corn, free of additives)

1 cup yellow tortilla chips (35 g)
(made from 100% corn)

PREPARATION TIME: approx. 15 minutes

Halve the **avocados,** remove the pits, and spoon out about 1½ cups (225 g) of avocado. Purée with **lemon juice** until smooth. Season with **salt** and **pepper**.

Mix the **cashew butter** together with the **mineral water** and **nutritional yeast flakes,** and season with **salt**. Remove the core from the **bell peppers,** wash, and cut into fine strips. Wash and clean the **chili pepper** and **scallion,** and cut both into fine strips.

Place the **tortilla chips** on a plate with the bell pepper strips. Using a spoon, form the avocado cream into egg-shaped portions. Top the chips with cashew cheese and garnish with the scallion and chili pepper strips.

AH! "These tortilla chips don't contain any artificial flavors or fatty laboratory cheese. Cashew cheese and avocados provide us with important nutrients, vitamins, minerals, and healthy fats. The bell peppers give us a Vitamin C kick. Eat as soon as possible; otherwise the chips will get mushy!"

QUINOA SALAD TO GO

INGREDIENTS for 2 people

Quinoa Salad:

1¼ cups quinoa (200 g)

Iodized sea salt

1 head of broccoli

3 carrots

¾ cup frozen peas (90 g)

2 scallions

1 red chili pepper

3 tablespoons olive oil

1 tablespoon chopped fresh mint

2 teaspoons lime juice

Grated peel of ½ organic lime

Freshly ground black pepper

Curry Sunflower Seeds:

3½ tablespoons sunflower seeds (30 g)

½ teaspoon curry powder

1 tablespoon olive oil

½ teaspoon agave syrup

Iodized sea salt

AH! "Use two separate containers: one for the salad, the other for the toasted seeds so that they don't get mushy. The salad will definitely be crisp and fresh and will make your colleagues green with envy!"

PREPARATION TIME: approx. 25 minutes

In a fine sieve, rinse the quinoa off with water. Pour into a small saucepan with just under 2¼ cups (530 mL) of water and ½ teaspoon sea salt. Cook uncovered over high heat approx. 17 minutes, until the liquid is absorbed. In the meantime, wash the broccoli, and cut just under 2½ cups (180 g) of florets from the stalk. Peel and slice the carrots into fine strips. Heat a large saucepan of salted water and cook the peas for 2 minutes. Add the broccoli and carrots and cook for another 2 minutes. Allow to drain in a sieve. Wash and clean the scallions and chili pepper, and cut into fine rings.

For the salad dressing, mix 2 tablespoons of olive oil together with the mint, lime juice, and lime peel. Season with salt and pepper to taste. Heat 1 tablespoon olive oil in a skillet and sauté the pre-cooked vegetables approx. 2 minutes. Mix the vegetables, spring onions and chili pepper together with the quinoa in a large bowl. Fold in the dressing, salt and pepper, and if desired, top with a dash of olive oil. Toast the sunflower seeds with the curry powder and 1 tablespoon olive oil in a small skillet over high heat for about 2 minutes. Add the agave syrup, remove from heat, and add salt. Sprinkle with sunflower seeds and serve on plates.

SWEET HIGHLIGHTS

The idea behind the rewards. You will notice that using a rewards system when you are on a diet and rigorous exercise program simply works wonders. For example, say to yourself: "Today I'll bike for an hour, but I'll also make myself pralines and eat a few after exercising." People aren't too complicated, and during these tough 30 days, you'll often feel that it's these small culinary highlights that keep you motivated.

The reward recipes on the following pages are optimized in terms of their ingredients—they are sweet treats, but it isn't a sin to eat them. They're actually good for the body, mind, and motivation. And you'll notice that you feel satisfied after just a few bites. It's often ingredients like industrial sugar and unhealthy animal fats, which make us feel like eating too much.

RECIPES FOR
REWARDS

CASHEW PANNA COTTA WITH STRAWBERRY SAUCE

INGREDIENTS for 4 servings

Panna Cotta:

4½ tablespoons cashew butter (70 g)

4 pinches ground Bourbon vanilla

4 tablespoons agave syrup (60 g)

½ teaspoon agar agar (1 g)

1 pinch iodized sea salt

Strawberry Sauce:

1⅓ cups strawberries (150 g)

2 tablespoons agave syrup (30 mL)

1 pinch iodized sea salt

2 pinches ground vanilla

In addition:

¾ cup blueberries for garnish (100 g)

PREPARATION TIME: approx. 20 minutes plus approx. 60 minutes cooling time

Mix together the **cashew butter, Bourbon vanilla, agave syrup, agar agar, sea salt** and just under 1¼ cups (280 mL) water in a blender at high speed until smooth. Pour the mixture into a small saucepan and bring to a boil, stirring constantly, and cook approx. 20 seconds. Pour mixture into 4 custard cups. Cover with parchment paper and set in the freezer for about 1 hour.

For the sauce, wash and clean the **strawberries.** Purée all **ingredients.**

Using a knife, loosen the panna cotta from the edge of the custard cups and let fall onto dessert plates. Pour the strawberry sauce on top. Wash the **blueberries,** remove any damaged berries, and garnish the panna cotta with the berries.

AH! "Cashews are rich in tryptophan, which our body uses to produce serotonin, and serotonin makes us happy. You can find cashew butter at organic grocery stores. Or you can also simply snack on cashew nuts. The creaminess of the panna cotta is unbeatable. You do need to make sure to use the right amount of agar agar. I recommend you weigh it precisely on an electronic scale!"

MINI CHOCOLATE COFFEE TART

INGREDIENTS for 8 pieces

Crust:

1½ teaspoons agave syrup (7 g)

¼ cup roasted hazelnuts (30 g)

½–⅔ cup roasted almonds (70 g)

6 dates (60 g)

1 pinch iodized sea salt

Coffee Cream:

1 tablespoon sunflower oil

14 ounces soft plain tofu (400 g)

½ teaspoon ground cinnamon

1 teaspoon ground decaffeinated
coffee beans

⅓ cup agave syrup (95 g)

1 tablespoon organic cocoa (7 g)

Chocolate Topping:

1 ounce cocoa butter (30 g)

1 pinch iodized sea salt

2 pinches ground vanilla

5 teaspoons agave syrup (25 g)

5 teaspoons organic cocoa (13 g)

4 teaspoons white almond butter
(20 g)

⅓–½ cup roasted hazelnuts (50 g)

PREPARATION TIME: approx. 35 minutes
plus approx. 30 minutes cooling time

Purée all of the ingredients for the crust, except for
the agave syrup, in a blender so that the hazelnuts
and almonds are ground into a powder. Add the
agave syrup and knead everything together until
you have a sticky dough.

Line the bottom of a springform pan (Diameter
7 inches (18 cm)) with parchment paper and
then snap the top part of the pan on top, letting
the parchment paper stick out under the sides.
Distribute the dough mixture evenly in the pan
and press out with the palms of your hands.

For the coffee cream, purée all the ingredients in
a strong blender until creamy.

For the topping, melt the cocoa butter over a
water bath. Fold in the salt, vanilla, agave syrup,
cocoa, and white almond butter with a whisk.
Chop the hazelnuts and add these to the mixture.
Spread the coffee cream out evenly on the crust
and pour the chocolate topping over the top. Set
in the refrigerator to chill approx. 30 minutes.

AH! "Sometimes it can take up to 10
minutes to purée the coffee cream if
your blender isn't too strong, but it
will still usually work."

WHOLE GRAIN RICE PUDDING WITH CHERRIES

INGREDIENTS for 2–3 people

Whole Grain Rice Pudding:

1 cup short-grain brown rice (200 g)

1¾–2 cups oat milk (450 mL)

1 level teaspoon ground vanilla

4 teaspoons agave syrup (20 g)

Cherries:

3⅔ cups frozen sour cherries (560 g)

2½ tablespoons agave syrup (40 g)

½ teaspoon agar agar

PREPARATION TIME: approx. 75 minutes

Place the **short-grain rice** with the **oat milk** and **vanilla** in a small saucepan and bring to a boil. Simmer over low heat approx. 70 minutes, stirring occasionally. The saucepan should be partially covered. Sweeten with **agave syrup,** adding additional **oat milk** if you wish to make the rice creamier.

In the meantime, heat the **sour cherries** and **agave syrup** in a small saucepan. Drain cherries in a sieve and collect the juice. Mix the **agar agar** with 3 tablespoons cold water. Add this mixture to the cherry juice and briefly bring to a boil in a small saucepan. **Sweeten** to taste and mix with the cherries.

To serve, layer the rice pudding with the cherries in a jar.

AH! "Prepare the rice the evening before. But make sure to set the timer; otherwise, the rice might start to burn—that's happened to me a bazillion times. And rice pudding also works great as a to-go snack. Brown rice hasn't been through the refining process and contains many essential minerals and vitamins. If you cook it long enough, it tastes just as creamy as the white rice used to make a less healthy version of rice pudding."

A. HAZEL CHOCOLATE PRALINES
B. COCONUT ALMOND COOLER
C. PEANUT CHOCOLATE CRUNCH
D. CINNAMON BLISS KISS

A

B

C

D

A. Hazel Chocolate Pralines

INGREDIENTS for approx. 22 pieces

Praline Mixture:

1⅔ cups roasted hazelnuts (200 g)

½ teaspoon ground vanilla

1 pinch iodized sea salt

3 tablespoons agave syrup (50 g)

2 teaspoons organic cocoa (5 g)

Chocolate Coating:

⅓ cup roasted hazelnuts (40 g)

4 ounces cocoa butter (120 g)

2 pinches ground vanilla

¼ cup agave syrup (60 g)

2½ tablespoons organic cocoa (20 g)

1 pinch iodized sea salt

PREPARATION TIME: approx. 20 minutes plus approx. 30 minutes cooling time

In a blender, coarsely grind just over ¾ cup (100 g) **hazelnuts** and finely grind just over ¾ cup (100 g) **hazelnuts**. Mix with the other **ingredients** for the praline mixture and form into small balls. Allow to cool approx. 20 minutes in the freezer. For the chocolate coating, coarsely grind the **hazelnuts** in a blender. Heat the **cocoa butter** in a small saucepan, mix in the remaining **ingredients** for the chocolate coating, and stir. Pour into a small bowl and let sit in the freezer approx. 10 minutes. Dip the pralines in the slightly thickened liquid chocolate; then allow to cool on a wire rack. You might want to dip the pralines twice, if the chocolate is too runny.

B. Coconut Almond Cooler

INGREDIENTS for approx. 22 pieces

⅓–½ cup whole peeled almonds (60 g)

1¼ cups unsweetened shredded coconut (90 g)

6½ tablespoons white almond butter (100 g)

2 tablespoons agave syrup (30 g)

1 pinch iodized sea salt

2 pinches ground vanilla

PREPARATION TIME: approx. 20 minutes

Grind the **almonds** and half of the **unsweetened shredded coconut** in a blender. Mix together with the rest of the **ingredients** to make a dough. Roll into balls.

C. Peanut Chocolate Crunch

INGREDIENTS for approx. 30 pieces

1 cup crunchy peanut butter (270 g)

2½ tablespoons organic cocoa (20 g)

⅓ cup agave syrup (80 g)

2 pinches ground vanilla

½ cup popped amaranth (20 g)

PREPARATION TIME: approx. 5 minutes plus approx. 15 minutes cooling time

Mix together the **peanut butter, cocoa, agave syrup,** and **vanilla** until smooth. Fold in the popped **amaranth**, form into pralines, and let cool in the refrigerator approx. 15 minutes.

D. Cinnamon Bliss Kiss

INGREDIENTS for approx. 20 pieces

1 cup popped amaranth (40 g)

½–⅔ cup cashew butter (140 g)

3 tablespoons agave syrup (50 g)

1 pinch iodized sea salt

½ teaspoon ground cinnamon

PREPARATION TIME: approx. 10 minutes plus approx. 10 minutes cooling time

Mix together all **ingredients** in a bowl with a fork. Roll into balls and then set in the freezer to cool for about 10 minutes.

LOW-CARB TARTLETS WITH STRAWBERRIES AND COCONUT WHIPPED CREAM

INGREDIENTS for 4 pieces

Low-Carb Tartlets:

3⅓ cups blanched almonds (400 g)

½ teaspoon ground vanilla

3 tablespoons agave syrup (50 g)

1 pinch iodized sea salt

2 pinches ground vanilla

Topping:

1⅓ cups strawberries (150 g)

¾ cup orange juice (180 mL)

¼ cup agave syrup (60 g)

½ teaspoon agar agar

Coconut Whipped Cream:

1 cup coconut milk cream (200 g)

5 teaspoons agave syrup (25 g)

2½ tablespoons white almond butter (40 g)

2 pinches ground vanilla

1 pinch iodized sea salt

In addition:

¼ cup chopped pistachios (30 g)

PREPARATION TIME: approx. 30 minutes plus approx. 30 minutes cooling time

For the tartlets, finely grind the almonds in a blender and then knead together with the other ingredients to make a smooth dough. Lightly grease four tartlet pans. Press the dough into the pans with your hands, and then carefully remove the pressed dough from the pans.

For the topping, wash the strawberries and remove the leaf-like caps. Cut the berries into quarters, and arrange the pieces on the tartlets.

Whisk together the orange juice, agave syrup, and agar agar; bring to a boil in a small saucepan and allow to cook for 30 seconds. Afterwards, place in the refrigerator for 10 minutes. Then spread the mixture over the strawberries. Let the tartlets cool in the refrigerator for 15 minutes.

Shortly before serving, mix together all of the ingredients (they should be at room temperature) for the whipped cream with an immersion blender for about 1 minute, until the mixture is smooth and no longer crumbly. Then use an electric hand mixer with beaters to mix for about 2 minutes, until the whipped cream is light and airy. Top the tartlets with the whipped cream and chopped pistachios.

AH! "Use the whipped cream immediately and don't put it back in the refrigerator because then it will get hard and take on a crumbly consistency."

VEGAN FOR FIT CHOCOLATE

INGREDIENTS for 1 big bar

3 ounces cocoa butter (90 g)

6 tablespoons white almond butter (95 g)

¼ cup organic cocoa (30 g)

2½ tablespoons agave syrup (40 g)

2 pinches ground vanilla

1 pinch iodized sea salt

PREPARATION TIME: approx. 15 minutes plus approx. 40 minutes cooling time

Melt the cocoa butter over a water bath. Remove from heat, and fold in the other ingredients with a whisk. Pour chocolate into a non-stick rectangular or similar type pan, set in the freezer approx. 10 minutes, and then set in the refrigerator for 30 minutes.
Dive in and enjoy.
Variations: add 50 g of pistachios, banana chips, roasted hazelnuts, goji berries, or roasted almonds.

Attila's White Chocolate

White Chocolate

3.5 ounces cocoa butter (100 g)

6½ tablespoons white almond butter (100 g)

3 tablespoons agave syrup (50 g)

1 level teaspoon ground vanilla

⅓ cup cranberries (50 g)

Melt the cocoa butter melt over a water bath. Remove from heat and add in the other ingredients, except the cranberries. Stir with a whisk and pour into a chocolate mold. Sprinkle the cranberries on top and let cool completely.

AH! "High-quality organic cocoa, almond butter and agave syrup as a sweetener. This is how you get chocolate that tastes like milk chocolate and it's also healthy. You can nibble on this chocolate with a good conscience."

LEMON CREAM CAKE WITH RASPBERRY SAUCE

INGREDIENTS for 12 pieces

Crust:

2½ cups roasted almonds (300 g)

7 pitted dates (70 g) (not sweetened with glucose syrup)

1 pinch iodized sea salt

1 level teaspoon ground vanilla

4 teaspoons agave syrup (20 g)

Cream Filling:

2 organic lemons

4 ounces cocoa butter (110 g)

2 cups white almond butter (500 g)

6½ tablespoons unsweetened cashew butter (100 g)

9½ tablespoons agave syrup (140 g)

3 tablespoons lecithin powder (30 g)

1 pinch iodized sea salt

Raspberry Sauce and Topping:

2¼ cups raspberries (250 g)

¾ cup blueberries (100 g)

1 cup strawberries (100 g)

⅓ cup blackberries (50 g)

2 tablespoons agave syrup

AH! "You can get lecithin powder online or at an organic grocery store. I don't buy the granules, but rather pure lecithin powder. By the way, if you want to save some money, you can make half a batch of the cream filling."

PREPARATION TIME: approx. 30 minutes plus approx. 12 hours cooling time

For the crust, place all of the ingredients, except for the agave syrup, into a blender and purée until the almonds are ground to a powder. Add the agave syrup and then knead until you have a sticky dough. Put the dough into a springform pan (Diameter 9 inches (23 cm), with a removable ring) lined with parchment paper and press the dough out with the palms of your hands.

For the filling, wash the lemons with hot water and dry. Grate the peel of 1 lemon, and then squeeze both lemons to make just under ½ cup (110 mL) juice. Purée the lemon peel and juice in a blender until smooth. In a small saucepan, melt the cocoa butter over a water bath over medium heat. Mix all of the ingredients for the filling together with 1¼ cups (300 mL) water in a strong kitchen blender until the mixture is smooth. Spread the mixture on the crust until it is nice and smooth, cover with parchment paper, and let stand in the freezer approx. 1 hour. Afterwards, let stand covered in the refrigerator overnight, until the mixture has set.

For the topping, sort out the damaged berries, wash and clean the good ones, and quarter the strawberries. Purée 1¾ cups (200 g) raspberries with agave syrup in a blender and then press the mixture through a fine sieve.

Spread the raspberry sauce on the lemon cake and top with the berries. Enjoy alongside a Matcha Latte.

A. PINEAPPLE FAT-BURNER ICE CREAM
B. CASHEW CHOCOLATE CHIP ICE CREAM

(For recipes, see pages 192–193.)

C. CHOCOLATE PEANUT BUTTER ICE CREAM
D. BANANA CINNAMON ICE CREAM
E. HAZELNUT CHOCOLATE ICE CREAM
F. STRAWBERRY ALMOND KISS

A. Pineapple Fat-Burner Ice Cream

INGREDIENTS for 2–3 scoops

1 pineapple

3 tablespoons agave syrup (50 g)

PREPARATION TIME: approx. 2 minutes plus approx. 12 hours cooling time

Peel the pineapple, halve lengthwise, and remove the stalk. Cut the pineapple into small cubes until you have 2 cups (400 g) and freeze overnight. Purée with the agave syrup.

B. Cashew Chocolate Chip Ice Cream

INGREDIENTS for 2–3 scoops

¾ cup cashew butter (200 g)

2 cups ice cubes (260 g)

2 pinches ground vanilla

1 pinch sea salt

3 tablespoons agave syrup (50 g)

1.7 ounces Vegan for Fit Chocolate (50 g)
(For recipe, see page 186)

PREPARATION TIME: approx. 5 minutes plus approx. 30 minutes cooling time

Purée all ingredients, except for the chocolate. Coarsely chop the chocolate and fold into the ice cream. Place the ice cream in the freezer approx. 30 minutes.

AH! "For me, it's a dream come true: healthy ice cream in just a few minutes—without the hassle of using an ice cream machine and without having to wait such a long time! For the perfect consistency, I recommend using a heavy duty blender with a tamper, such as the Vitamix."

C. CHOCOLATE PEANUT BUTTER ICE CREAM
D. BANANA CINNAMON ICE CREAM

(For photo, see page 190.)

C. Chocolate Peanut Butter Ice Cream

INGREDIENTS for 2–3 scoops

¾ cup peanut butter (200 g)

2 cups ice cubes (260 g)

4 tablespoons agave syrup (65 g)

1 pinch iodized sea salt

½ teaspoon ground vanilla

5 tablespoons organic cocoa (40 g)

PREPARATION TIME: approx. 5 minutes plus approx. 20 minutes cooling time

Mix the **peanut butter, ice cubes, agave syrup, sea salt,** and **vanilla** thoroughly. Take out half the mixture and mix with **cocoa.** Stir both mixtures slightly with a fork, so that they both look marbled. Set in the freezer for approx. 20 minutes to cool.

D. Banana Cinnamon Ice Cream

INGREDIENTS for 2–3 scoops

Approx. 2 bananas

3 tablespoons cashew butter (50 g)

2 tablespoons agave syrup (30 g)

1 pinch iodized sea salt

½ teaspoon ground cinnamon

PREPARATION TIME: approx. 2 minutes plus approx. 12 hours cooling time

Peel the ripe **bananas,** cut them in quarters, and place them (300 g) in a freezer overnight. Purée with the other **ingredients.**

E. HAZELNUT CHOCOLATE ICE CREAM
F. STRAWBERRY ALMOND KISS

(For photo, see page 190.)

E. Hazelnut Chocolate Ice Cream

INGREDIENTS for 2–4 scoops

¾ cup hazelnut butter (200 g)

2–2¼ cups ice cubes (270 g)

4½ tablespoons agave syrup (70 g)

5 teaspoons organic cocoa (13 g)

1 pinch iodized sea salt

½ teaspoon ground vanilla

PREPARATION TIME: approx. 2 minutes plus approx. 15 minutes cooling time

Purée all ingredients. Then set in the freezer approx. 15 minutes.

F. Strawberry Almond Kiss

INGREDIENTS for 2–3 scoops

Approx. 3⅔ cups strawberries (approx. 400 g)

¼ cup agave syrup (60 g)

⅓ cup white almond butter (80 g)

½ teaspoon ground vanilla

PREPARATION TIME: approx. 2 minutes plus approx. 12 hours cooling time

Wash and clean the strawberries. Place 2⅔ cups (300 g) clean strawberries in the freezer overnight. Combine all the ingredients in a blender and purée to a smooth ice cream. You may then, optionally, set the mixture in the freezer for a short while.

YOGURT MANDARIN CAKE
WITH AMARANTH CRUST

INGREDIENTS for 8 pieces

Crust:

⅔ cup roasted almonds (75 g)

1¼ cups popped amaranth (50 g)

4½ tablespoons agave syrup (70 g)

2 pinches ground vanilla

1 pinch iodized sea salt

2½ tablespoons dark almond butter (40 g)

Yogurt Filling:

6 mandarins

8 teaspoons agar agar (16 g)

½ cup agave syrup (130 g)

5⅓ cups soy yogurt (1.2 kg)

Glaze:

¾ cup canned mandarins (175 g) (without added sugar, drained)

4 mandarins

½ teaspoon agar agar

AH! "You can bake the cake the evening before and then let it cool overnight. Here, too, you need to make sure that you have the exact amount of agar agar and that you stir it in quickly; otherwise, the cake won't set properly and it'll have lots of strange-looking lumps."

PREPARATION TIME: approx. 30 minutes plus approx. 60 minutes cooling time

Finely grind the roasted almonds in a kitchen blender. Mix all of the ingredients for the crust with a fork. Line the bottom of a springform pan (Diameter 9 inches (23 cm)) with parchment paper, place the dough into the pan, and press out evenly.

For the filling, squeeze just over ¾ cup (approx. 200 mL juice) of juice from the mandarins. Stir the mandarin juice, agar agar, and agave syrup quickly to avoid lumps from forming. Bring to a boil in a small saucepan, remove from the heat, and then quickly fold in the yogurt with a whisk. Spread the yogurt mixture on the crust and set in the freezer for approx. 30 minutes.

For the glaze, drain the canned mandarins and then arrange them in a circular pattern on top of the cake. Squeeze the juice from the fresh mandarins (makes about ⅔ cup or 150 mL), and mix with the agar agar in a small saucepan. Cook approx. 30 seconds while stirring with a whisk. Pour the juice on top of the cake that is still in the springform pan and then put it back in the freezer for 30 minutes or in the refrigerator for 40 minutes.

COCONUT CHOCOLATE BARS

INGREDIENTS for 10 bars

Coconut Bars:

10 cups coconut flakes (300 g)

¼ cup agave syrup (60 g)

1 pinch iodized sea salt

½ cup coconut milk cream

from 1 can of coconut milk (90 g)

Chocolate Coating:

4 ounces cocoa butter (120 g)

½ cup white almond butter (120 g)

½ cup organic cocoa (60 g)

¼ cup agave syrup (60 g)

1 pinch iodized sea salt

4 pinches ground vanilla

AH! "It's important that you don't confuse coconut milk cream with coconut oil. What the recipe calls for is the coconut milk cream that separates out and rises to the top of organic coconut milk, and not the more transparent coconut oil, which you can buy in jars and use for frying. In conventional coconut milk, the cream doesn't separate out because chemical additives such as emulsifiers are used to make sure that everything remains liquid."

PREPARATION TIME: approx. 30 minutes plus approx. 15 minutes cooling time

Grind the **coconut flakes** in a blender until they are medium fine. Mix together with the remaining **ingredients** for the bars with a fork. Shape the mixture together with your hands into 10 chocolate bars. Place the bars onto a plate lined with parchment paper and let stand in the freezer for 10 minutes.

For the chocolate coating, melt the **cocoa butter** over a water bath. Remove from heat and fold in the remaining **ingredients** for the coating with a whisk. Take the coconut bars out of the freezer and place them on a wire rack. Put a piece of parchment paper under the rack. Spoon the chocolate mixture onto the bars, coating all sides of the bars by using the back of a spoon or a brush. Make the wave form in the chocolate bars using the back of a spoon. Put the bars back into the freezer for another 5 minutes on a piece of parchment paper. After that, the bars are ready to snack on. It's best to store them in the refrigerator.

GREAT DRINKS

The human body is composed of 70 percent water. Drinking enough is therefore essential—particularly in periods of physical exertion, such as during the Challenge. Along with about 2–3 liters of high-quality organic mineral water, I also drink a lot of infused green tea, superfood drinks, and matcha shakes because they provide me with phytonutrients and give me a lot of energy for the day. Green tea does take a bit of getting used to. So, in the next section, you'll find recipes for amazing tasting green tea shakes. Coffee only perks me up for a short time; in contrast, the effects of green tea last much longer because it contains both caffeine and theobromine. And green tea will noticeably inhibit your appetite.

RECIPES FOR
DRINKS

SHAKES TO FLY
A. SUPERFOOD SHAKE
B. APPLE ORANGE GINGER SHAKE
C. SILKEN TOFU AND CINNAMON SHAKE

A. Superfood Shake

INGREDIENTS for 1 shake

1½ tablespoons goji berries (10 g)

4½ tablespoons acai juice (70 mL)

¾–1 cup raspberries (100 g)

½ cup blueberries (60 g)

2½ tablespoons agave syrup (40 g)

1½ tablespoons white almond butter (20 g)

⅔ cup non-carbonated mineral water (150 mL)

B. Apple Orange Ginger Shake

INGREDIENTS for 1 shake

Just over 2 cups orange juice (260 mL)

1 one-inch cube peeled ginger (8 g)

⅔ cup peeled and cored apple (70 g)

2 tablespoons lime juice

4 teaspoons agave syrup (20 g)

⅔ cup ice cubes (80 g)

C. Silken Tofu and Cinnamon Shake

INGREDIENTS for 1 shake

7 ounces silken tofu (200 g)

¾ cup ice cubes (100 g)

4 teaspoons agave syrup (20 g)

1 teaspoon ground cinnamon

1 pinch iodized sea salt

PREPARATION TIME PER SHAKE: approx. 3 minutes

For each shake, blend all ingredients thoroughly, pour into a glass, and serve.

SAMURAI SHAKES
A. MATCHA BANANA CHOCOLATE SHAKE
B. MATCHARIÑHA
C. MATCHA VANILLA ALMOND MILK

A. Matcha Banana Chocolate Shake

INGREDIENTS for 1 shake

1¼ cups oat milk (300 mL)

3 tablespoons white almond butter (50 g)

2 tablespoons agave syrup

2 pinches ground vanilla

1 slightly rounded teaspoon matcha

2 slightly rounded teaspoons organic cocoa

1 small banana (70 g)

5 ice cubes

PREPARATION TIME: approx. 3 minutes
Thoroughly blend all the ingredients together except for the ice cubes. Put the ice cubes in a glass and then pour the shake on top.

B. Matchariñha

INGREDIENTS for 1 shake

2 organic limes

Just over 1 cup non-carbonated, cold mineral water (250 mL)

1 level teaspoon matcha

4 tablespoons agave syrup (60 g)

5 ice cubes

PREPARATION TIME: approx. 3 minutes
Cut 1 lime in half and squeeze the juice out (approx. 3 tablespoons or 40 mL of juice). Mix thoroughly with the mineral water, matcha, and agave syrup. Wash 1 lime, dry, and cut into quarters. Put the ice cubes in a glass and fill it up with the Matcha Lime mix.

C. Matcha Vanilla Almond Milk

INGREDIENTS for 1 shake

1¼ cups almond milk (300 mL)

1 pinch iodized sea salt

1½ tablespoons agave syrup

4 pinches ground vanilla

1 slightly rounded teaspoon matcha

5 ice cubes

PREPARATION TIME: approx. 3 minutes
Mix all of the ingredients except for the ice cubes thoroughly. Put the ice cubes in a glass and then pour the shake on top.

A

B

C

GREEN BOOSTER
A. GREEN TEA CHERRY POP
B. GREEN TEA GINGER MINGER
(For recipe, see pages 206–207)
C. GREEN TEA CREAM
D. GREEN TEA COCONUT FLOW
E. GREEN TEA POMEGRANATE
F. GREEN TEA OJ

INGREDIENTS for 1 glass

2–3 tea bags of green tea

⅔ cup boiling water (150 mL)

BASIC RECIPE

Pour water over strong green tea (See each recipe for the specific amount), except for in the case of the Green Tea Cherry Pop recipe, and then let steep approx. 5–10 minutes so that the phytonutrients can be drawn out—in contrast to the common belief that it is better to take the tea bag out sooner.

Mix with the respective ingredients. For cold variations, allow the tea to chill in the freezer, and serve with as many ice cubes as you like.

A. **Green Tea Cherry Pop**

INGREDIENTS for 1 glass

5 mint leaves

⅔ cup green tea (150 mL)

½ cup cherry juice (120 mL)

4 teaspoons agave syrup (20 g)

5 ice cubes

PREPARATION TIME: approx. 2 minutes plus approx. 30 minutes chilling time

Brew the green tea with the mint leaves, and then let chill—as described in the basic recipe. Mix all of the other ingredients with the tea and serve ice cold.

B. **Green Tea Ginger Minger**

INGREDIENTS for 1 glass

1 small piece of ginger

2½ tablespoons lemon juice (40 mL)

Grated peel of ½ organic lemon

3 tablespoons agave syrup (50 g)

1 cup hot green tea (250 mL)

PREPARATION TIME: approx. 5 minutes

Peel the ginger and cut into thin slices. Mix all of the ingredients together with the green tea and serve hot.

C. GREEN TEA CREAM
D. GREEN TEA COCONUT FLOW

(Photo on page 204)

C. Green Tea Cream

INGREDIENTS for 1 glass

6 tablespoons oat milk (90 mL)

1 pinch ground vanilla

2 tablespoons agave syrup (30 g)

1 cup hot green tea (250 mL)

PREPARATION TIME: approx. 2 minutes

Mix all of the **ingredients** together with the **green tea** and serve hot.

D. Green Tea Coconut Flow

INGREDIENTS for 1 glass

½ cup hot coconut milk (120 mL)

4 teaspoons agave syrup (20 g)

1 cup hot green tea (250 mL)

PREPARATION TIME: approx. 7 minutes

Mix all of the **ingredients** together with the **green tea** and serve hot.

E. GREEN TEA POMEGRANATE
F. GREEN TEA OJ

(Photo on page 204)

E. Green Tea Pomegranate

INGREDIENTS for 1 glass

6½ tablespoons pomegranate juice (100 mL)

2 tablespoons agave syrup (30 g)

4 teaspoons acai juice (20 mL)

5 ice cubes

A little less than 1 cup strong green tea (200 mL)

PREPARATION TIME: approx. 2 minutes plus approx. 30 minutes chilling time
Mix all of the **ingredients** together with the **green tea** and serve ice cold.

F. Green Tea OJ

INGREDIENTS for 1 glass

1 organic orange

⅓ cup orange juice (80 mL)

2½ tablespoons agave syrup (40 g)

5 ice cubes

⅓ cup strong green tea (80 mL)

PREPARATION TIME: approx.5 minutes plus approx. 30 minutes chilling time
Wash the **orange** with hot water, dry, and halve. Cut one half into thin slices. Squeeze the juice from the other half and mix together with the **orange juice.** Mix all of the **ingredients** with the **green tea** and serve ice cold.

IN RESTAURANTS

WHEN YOU HAVE TO MAKE DO WITH
what's available—in restaurants

Luckily, most university and company cafeterias have a large salad bar, and they at least have a few vegan dishes on the menu. But the salad dressings available often leave something to be desired. So, it's best to prepare your own salad dressing at home and take it with you. You can make your salads more nutritious by adding fried tofu cubes or chopped and toasted nuts and seeds. However, things are changing. For example, The Free University of Berlin, where I studied, recently established the first vegetarian cafeteria at a German university. The vegan-vegetarian mindset has crept into academic circles, which naturally makes me very happy!

The situation is quite different in restaurants. If you are traveling with colleagues, then you, I'm sorry to say, are screwed. I'm on the road so often and it's unfortunately always the same. Even many fine restaurants have limited vegan offerings on the menu and these are often bland or lack creativity. One night, after a talk show, all they had for me was some plain asparagus and potatoes. And that was in a good restaurant. Fortunately, I had brought along some of my Best Snack Bars in the World, made with amaranth, and my constant companion—a jar of crunchy peanut butter and a banana. Still, I ate a piece of asparagus, just to be polite.

But what I would really like you to consider are organic restaurants and snack bars at organic grocery stores. You can easily find out where these are by taking a quick look on the internet with your smartphone. You'll find that there are many locations where the vegan offerings are really very diverse: there are soups, fresh salads, whole grain rolls with spreads, fresh fruit grown without pesticides, and sweet, healthy treats. I usually buy a ready-mixed salad and then boost the nutritional value by adding artichoke hearts from a jar, olives, or some sun-dried tomatoes; sprinkling a few roasted nuts and seeds over the top; and topping everything with crispy sprouts. For dessert, some sweet, fresh fruit and a tablespoon of cashew butter—then I'm full and satisfied!

Incidentally, the organic scene has long been connected to the vegetarian food culture. I think that's awesome and that's why these restaurants are always my first choice. What I also think is nice about organic snack bars and restaurants is that you can get the people who are with you excited about the Challenge because, as I said before, many organic restaurants have a delicious vegan menu. And if you live in the middle of nowhere and there is nothing close to you, then you probably have no other choice than to move to a bigger city or to open your own store. Yeah, how awesome would that be? Vegan Challenger restaurants in every city—and soon after, everybody would be a Challenger, fit and full of life, helping each other, and eating a diet based on the latest scientific findings. We should never stop dreaming!

LET'S GO

THIS IS DEFINITELY NOT ONE OF MY STANDARD EXERCISES.
BUT FOR THIS PICTURE, IT DID ACTUALLY WORK FOR JUST A MOMENT…

SETTING YOUR GOALS
You have to know what you want!

Before you even think about buying workout clothes, signing up for a gym, or completing this Challenge, it's very helpful to truly listen to yourself and ask yourself what you really want. Do you want to get fit, lose weight, improve your skin, detox, build more muscle, or get a firm butt?

Your goal should be as concrete as possible because only in this way will it be motivating. Nobody would be able to make it through a marathon if they didn't keep the finish line in mind as the goal that they definitely wanted to reach. So, write down what your own personal marathon finish line is!

The goals I had in the past seem almost like craziness today. At least, most people would see it that way—an overweight couch potato who makes it his goal to get on the cover of *Men's Health*. When I look at my body today and compare it with the body I had eleven years ago, I see a transformation that astonishes me even today. My skin has remained firm in spite of losing 35 kilograms and looking at the shape I was in back then, it's on the edge of being a miracle that I didn't have to have an operation. This was certainly because of my age and genes, but also because of the fruit and vegetables I consumed that contain vital substances, some of which have skin-firming properties, and because of my consistent approach to building up muscle. Now, I'm fit and look the way that I dreamed about back then. And I was able to reach my goals because I always kept this finish line in sight, just like my motto:

"If you reach for the stars, you'll often at least land on the moon."

And now I'm going to share a secret with you as to how you can achieve your goals this time: every time that you are feeling weak, ask yourself if this sin is worth not reaching your goal. Make it a habit to repeat this to yourself! Then, with awareness, decide in just a few seconds and don't think about it for even one second longer.

I believe that almost every goal can be achieved if you have experienced the power of this technique. So, we'll see each other on the cover of *Men's Health!*

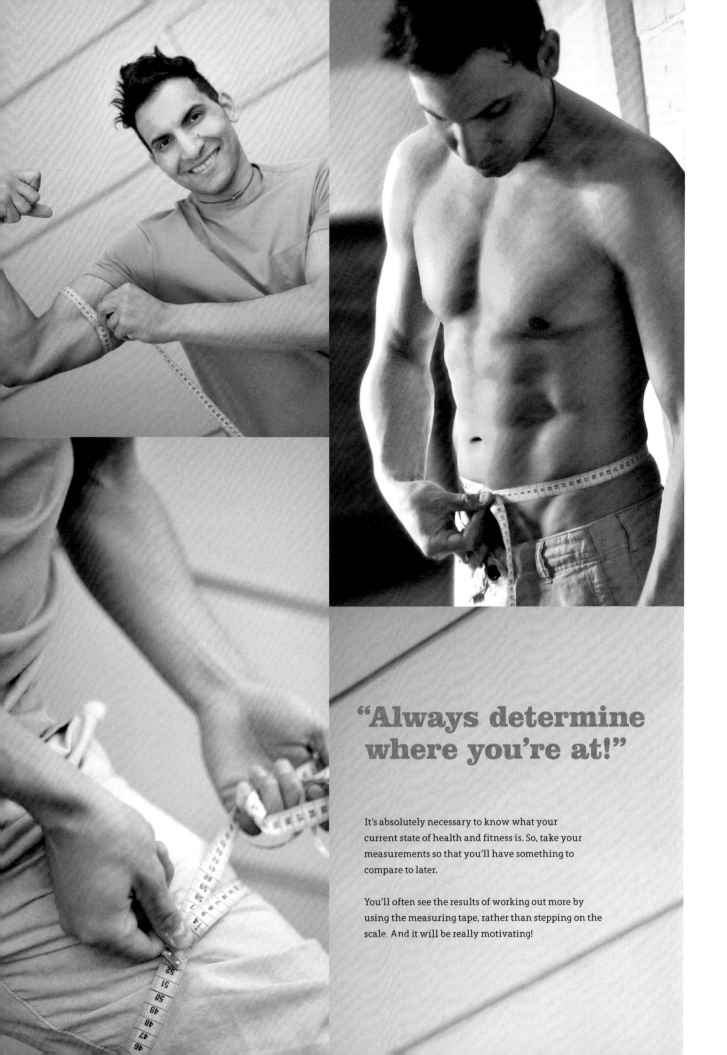

"Always determine where you're at!"

It's absolutely necessary to know what your current state of health and fitness is. So, take your measurements so that you'll have something to compare to later.

You'll often see the results of working out more by using the measuring tape, rather than stepping on the scale. And it will be really motivating!

DO YOU WANT TO LOSE WEIGHT?

If you want to lose weight, then it's best to buy a copy of *Vegan for Fit*. If you want to lose weight faster, then you should buy two copies and use them to do weight lifting exercises. OK, all joking aside, the basis for losing weight is a healthy diet that satisfies us and gives our body exactly what it needs. With these recipes, you're off to a good start.

Many of the first Challengers were unfortunately so busy with college, work, family, or school that they didn't have any time to work out. And yet they still achieved phenomenal results and lost a lot of weight—without feeling hungry! But if you want to lose weight faster, I recommend endurance sports.

With cycling, brisk walking, running, or swimming, you'll feel good, and at the same time, you'll burn calories and force your body to start using up its fat reserves. I'm a passionate city biker. I bike everywhere, and by doing so, I'm saving money and protecting the environment. And anyway, I can't stand to be stuck in a car in slow, city traffic—I'm far too impatient and need action on my bike. Nothing is better than taking a steep flight of stairs on a mountain bike every now and then; that gives me my daily adrenaline rush and helps me train my coordination. Or I'll take a shortcut through the city park and get some fresh air for a change. Whether it's spring, summer, autumn, or winter, it's only when I'm cycling that I really feel alive and feel that I am truly here! I can also gladly do without sweating to death in summer rush-hour traffic. Instead, when I'm biking, I feel the caress of the sun on my skin and the wind in my hair.

There is no way to get a firm butt faster than on a bike! You see, for me, riding my bike is the ideal way to achieve multiple things at once—for example, getting quickly from Point A to Point B while burning calories. And, it's pure freedom to be able to use the strength of your own body to get around.

So, dig your old bike out of the basement and get it checked at a bike shop to make sure it's in good working order. Or go out and buy yourself the bike that will make cycling fun for you.

DO YOU WANT
to get fit or build muscle?

There are no shortcuts to getting fit more quickly. Instead, any long-term program to get and stay fit includes healthy training that builds up as you go; training that challenges your body, but doesn't overwork it; time for recovery; and nutrient-rich foods. Crash diets are, in my opinion, as crazy as bulking up phases or unbalanced high-protein diets with chemical shakes and pills in order to build muscles faster.

I am often asked what I think about protein drinks. My answer is that these types of drinks are unwelcome both in my kitchen and in my stomach. The strongest animals in nature are herbivores, and they don't need any chemicals or protein drinks. The best shake for me will always be hard training and good sleep—period.

Most of these shakes don't have any fiber or vital substances and consist purely of chemically derived protein. And instead of having to get used to the taste of these shakes, I would much prefer to eat a banana dipped in peanut butter or to feast on some reward pralines.

I basically don't worry about protein anymore, which wasn't always the case. Years ago, I tried lots of varieties of protein shakes until I finally began to realize they weren't good for me. Tofu and lentils also have tons of protein. In addition, lentils contain a lot of iron: 8 mg per 100 g. And parsley has 97.8 mg per 100 g. Compared to that, pork with 3 mg of iron looks pretty bad. Firm tofu contains 17 grams of protein per 100 grams. A beef steak does contain a bit more with 22 g per 100 g, but it's suspected to cause colon cancer as it falls in the category of red meat. With a balanced vegan diet, you will be laying the foundation for your health and fitness, and you can optimize this with a well-structured training plan. It's not about how much you can press on the bench or how fast you run—having fun when you work out, just like enjoying your food when you eat, should be the most important thing

BLOOD TEST

It's important that you get your blood tested so that you can see where you're at. For this, it's best to go to your family doctor. Unfortunately, that costs money—unless you are feeling bad or sick. Then, of course, your doctor will need to do a blood test to find out why you are feeling so bad.

Your health insurance will usually pay for this. Did you just now buy *Vegan for Fit* because you're already doing really well? No? Well, you see, there we have it: you're feeling bad.

So, off to the doctor. The most interesting values are for uric acid, Vitamin B12 and Vitamin D, naturally your cholesterol levels, and possibly any evidence of an iron deficiency. If the blood test comes back with any abnormalities, you should discuss these with your doctor and see what you can do to take care of the problem. You shouldn't worry about your supply of vitamins during the Challenge: a balanced vegan diet is significantly richer in natural vitamins than most people's current diet. The only supplement you'll need to take is Vitamin B12, which you can do by consuming enriched products, just like you do, for example, with iodine via iodized salt. And anyway, the body has enough Vitamin B12 reserves to last for two full years. The rest is just fairy tales about how vegans look pale and sick.

After 30 days, it's best to get a second blood test done: your cholesterol and triglyceride values will most likely have significantly changed for the better.

GET YOUR SELF-DISCIPLINE BACK, GET UP, CLEAN UP, USE YOUR EXTRA ENERGY

If you can be consistent for 30 days, then you can flush out all of the toxins that we take in, thanks to the food industry. At the beginning, of course, it will be necessary to have a good amount of self-discipline. But the first 100 Challengers managed this surprisingly easily and quickly, and you can, too.

It's best that every day you just focus on that one particular day—until you have completed the 30 days. And the triumph will be an incredible feeling: a victory over the inner glutton, consistently eating healthy, cooking more consciously, and having gained more vitality with more fitness.

The goal: after a challenging run up the stairs, stand on top of the hill, feel full of energy, let the wind blow over your skin and through your hair, spread your arms out like an eagle, and say to yourself, "I did it! I won the battle with myself!" You should be able to use this extra energy in other areas of life and be able to really clean up. Nothing is more liberating than completely restarting your system. This isn't only the case for computers. Almost everyone has multiple problem areas in their lives, but with the newfound energy you have, you can start right away and change all the things that you have always wanted to change. So, in addition to greater fitness, it makes sense to set additional new goals for your life. With more energy, optimally powered cells, and being free from toxins, many things in life will simply be easier.

And as for the Challenge, you can extend it until you have reached your desired weight—to 60 days, 90 days, or longer, depending on how much weight you want to lose. I recommend concentrating on any weight problems in one long phase, going slowly and decreasing steadily, no matter how much it is. The start or restart is always the hardest, but already on Day Two it starts to get easier. So, just give it one more day: if you did it yesterday, you can do it today, too. And then tomorrow it will be a little easier.

In the long term, you can re-introduce more starchy products into your diet. And anyway, it's easier to maintain your weight when you are eating a vegan diet. Within one year, I lost the first 20 of 35 kilograms using the Vegan for Fun recipes. You can actually eat Italian pasta or chocolate mousse once in a while since both are lower in fat in their vegan versions. The chocolate mousse recipe in *Vegan for Fun* has 50 percent less fat than its counterpart that uses animal products.

Eating organic food is not more expensive in the long run. Once you get the basics like nut butter and matcha, the cost of fresh fruit and vegetables is quite low.

1.

2.

3.

EXERCISE COURSE
Warm-up and stretching

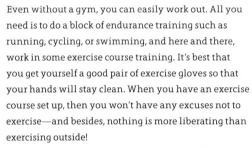

Even without a gym, you can easily work out. All you need is to do a block of endurance training such as running, cycling, or swimming, and here and there, work in some exercise course training. It's best that you get yourself a good pair of exercise gloves so that your hands will stay clean. When you have an exercise course set up, then you won't have any excuses not to exercise—and besides, nothing is more liberating than exercising outside!

Stretching relaxes your muscles and reduces the risk of injury. But don't stretch until after you have moved around a bit to get warm. Hold each stretch for about 30–60 seconds, longer if you like.

1. HAMSTRING STRETCH

Place your leg up on a high object, and grab your foot with your fingertips or at least get as close as you can. Alternatively, stand with straight legs, bend over, and try to touch your toes—if you put your legs closer together, you'll get a more intense stretch.

2. SHOULDER STRETCH

Stretch one arm out in front of your chest, hook the other arm around it, and pull it towards your chest until you feel a stretch.

3. CHEST STRETCH

Bend your arm at the elbow, place your forearm against an object for support, and then twist your body in the opposite direction until you feel a stretch.

4. QUADRICEPS STRETCH

Stand on one leg, bend the other leg at the knee, grab the foot with one hand, and pull towards your backside.

4.

1.

2.

3.

4.

STRENGTH
for the arms
and back

1.–3. PULL-UPS

Pull-ups help you build strong back muscles. These
are important because you probably sit much too long
and much too frequently in office chairs, which isn't
good for your back. A narrow grip primarily works
your arms and biceps. A wide grip helps you to work
the latissimus dorsi, commonly known as the lats. To
start, you should grab the bar so that you can see your
fingernails. This exercise is however very difficult, and
even one pull-up is a huge challenge for many people.
Slowly increase the number of repetitions and do as
many as you can.

4. DIPS FOR THE TRICEPS (THE BACK ARM MUSCLES)

Grab two parallel bars with your hands. Bend to a 90°
angle, and then return back to the starting position.

SAMPLE TRAINING PLAN

You should choose the times you exercise and your
rest days based on your current fitness level. You can
also exercise in the mornings and evenings so that you
split the exercises up, just make sure to do one muscle
group at a time. And if you only walk around the block
for 5 minutes because you've never exercised before,
well, that has just as much meaning as running a marathon. You can only reach your goal if you increase the
difficulty slowly and steadily. Your body will adapt—at
some point, you will feel the need to work out. You
may already start to feel this way even after the first
three days.

DAY 1: 60 minutes cycling and exercise course
training for the legs
DAY 2: 30 minutes swimming and exercise course
training for chest, triceps, and abdomen
DAY 3: Rest day
DAY 4: 30 minutes jogging and exercise course
training for the legs and abdomen
DAY 5: 30 minutes swimming and exercise course
training for the back and biceps
DAY 6: Rest day
DAY 7: Exercise course training for the abdomen
DAY 1: From here, it starts all over again...

1.

2.

3.

BALANCE
Strength for the legs and chest

1. CALF MUSCLES

With the balls of your foot on a step, lower slowly down into a stretch, and then come up as far as possible. It's best to begin by holding on to a railing and then later to do the exercise without any support.

2. SQUATS

Squats done without weights work the leg muscles completely. Bend your knees slowly, stop when you get to about 90 degrees, and then return to a standing position. Doing leg squats with one leg will train your coordination. When you are more advanced and want to strengthen your legs even more, you can do the same exercise holding dumbbells in your hands or hold the squat at 90 degrees for a few seconds, minutes, or—like the Shaolin monks—for a few hours.

3. PUSH-UPS

Push-ups are good for the chest muscles. The wider you place your hands, the more you train the outer chest and shoulder muscles. The narrower you place your hands, the more you work the inner chest and triceps. Doing push-ups at different angles, for example, with your legs on a bench, works different areas of the chest. Stop close to the floor, feel the tension, and then push up again. Do as many as you can and do multiple sets. For more weight, pros get their work-out partners to sit on their back or they keep their body tense and do the push-ups between two horizontal bars.

4. LUNGES

Doing lunges is the best way to get a firm butt: stand with your legs shoulder width apart, then take a big step forward with one leg, and go into a deep bend. Feel the tension and then go back to the starting position. Repeat the exercise with the other leg. Pros do the exercise standing in front of a tall object, such as a park bench—that will train your coordination and help you get a firm butt.

4.

1.

ABDOMINALS
Exercises for an 8-pack

1.–3. LEG RAISES

Leg raises train the lower abs and are essential for building an eight pack: at the beginning, start by lying on the ground with your hands at your sides, and then lift your legs up without bending your knees. For a more advanced workout, hang from a bar and lift your legs up out in front of you without bending your knees, and then lower them slowly in a controlled manner—raising them diagonally with your knees bent trains the lateral abdominal muscles. Start slowly at first, with your knees bent, then progress to where you can keep your legs straight. Pros put leg weights on and do the raises with straight legs or with a dumbbell between their legs, which they hold in place with their feet, and their knees bent.

4. CRUNCHES

Crunches work the upper abdominal muscles. Place your hands behind or alongside your head, bend your knees with your feet on the ground, rise up slightly just until you begin to feel tension, and then release back to the ground in a controlled manner.

ATTILA'S 10 GOLDEN RULES FOR LIFELONG HEALTHY TRAINING:

1. In the beginning, overcome your resistance and just get yourself out there. The first workouts are always exhausting.
2. After the initial success, the desire to keep working out will come about all by itself. Working out should be fun.
3. Always warm up and stretch both after warming up and working out.
4. Take enough time to recover and take rest days since you build muscle when you are recovering and resting.
5. Increase slowly—you can't start one day and participate in the Ironman triathlon the next!
6. Don't risk any injuries. If you do injure yourself, you could have setbacks for months.
7. Separate upper- and lower-body workouts as much as possible; that way you'll recover quicker.
8. Learn to listen to your body. It'll take a few weeks until you know what your body wants.
9. Never train when you have a cold. It's better to rest and drink green tea with ginger and lemon.
10. Never exercise if you are in pain. I mean real pain, not the aches and pains you get from working out.

DIET AND GROCERY SHOPPING
rules for the 30 days

Vegan for Fit offers a unique collection of really delicious and completely satisfying dishes that are free of all industrial additives and "prosperity poisons." In addition, the recipes provide a more balanced supply of proteins, fats, carbohydrates, natural vitamins, and phytonutrients than a typical diet possibly could. You will find that the recipes as a whole also work to counteract excess acidity in the body.

**YOU SHOULD KEEP THE FOLLOWING RULES DURING THE CHALLENGE
IF YOU WANT TO LOSE WEIGHT AND COMPLETELY RESET YOUR BODY:**

1. For the next 30 days, do your shopping in an organic grocery store or buy approved organic products, even if it initially seems more expensive. It's the only way that you can avoid consuming substances that just don't belong in food. Use the opportunity to get advice from employees in the store as they have a high level of expertise and gladly take time for every customer. Make sure they know that you only want to buy vegan products.

2. Eat breakfast and lunch until you are completely full. All of the recipes in this book will help you to prepare filling meals. After 4:00 p.m., only eat the recipes that are labeled "Level 1." During this time, eat only as much as necessary and as little as possible. After 7:00 p.m., try not to eat anything else. But you shouldn't go to bed with a grumbling stomach. These guidelines are, of course, only for those who have a typical daily schedule—if you work shifts or nights or have other time constraints, eat at mealtimes that work for you. The main point is that you shouldn't load your body down so much with digestion before going to bed. It's easier to lose weight quickly if you eat less at night because we don't feel hungry when we are asleep and then our bodies can begin to use our fat reserves, without it disturbing us so much.

3. Eat lots of fruits and vegetables. Just eat a smaller amount of those that are calorie and carbohydrate-rich such as bananas, dried fruit, grapes, avocados, and raisins.

4. If you need a snack or you're craving something, eat a small handful of nuts or 3–4 teaspoons nut butter, vegetable sticks with hummus, or a few Challenger pralines (See the chapter titled "Sweet Highlights. The idea behind the rewards.").

5. Greatly reduce the amount of starchy foods you eat: pasta, white bread, flour, potatoes, fries, and white rice aren't allowed, even if they are vegan.

6. Do not eat any animal products—no milk, eggs, cheese, cream, ice cream, gummy bears, or fish.

7. Do not drink any sugary drinks such as soft drinks. And don't drink any juice because it contains less fiber than fruit.

8. Use agave syrup, coconut palm sugar, natural apple syrup, and Stevia (the latter in small amounts, otherwise, it doesn't taste good) as sweeteners; don't use industrial sugar or raw cane sugar.

9. Do not buy any convenience foods (processed foods). Some exceptions are allowed such as canned tomatoes or frozen peas when fresh tomatoes or peas are not in season.

10. One recommendation: drink 1.5 liters of green tea (unsweetened or one of the recipes in this book) throughout the day. Green tea has a bit of a euphoric effect, and it reduces hunger pangs that you might have since it's a natural appetite suppressor.

11. Coffee is allowed, but not recommended. Going without cigarettes and alcohol makes the Challenge perfect. If you can't drop them completely the first day, then reduce a little bit each day. Many people manage to give these up altogether after only a few days! Still today, cruel animal tests are being conducted for cigarettes. This is perverse and absurd and another reason to ditch the cancer sticks. And anyway, smoking is not cool; you are only greatly increasing your risk of getting cancer. Alcohol belongs to the group of neurotoxins. However, I do really like to use red wine for cooking—the alcohol evaporates, and only the flavor remains.

MOTIVATION

HERE'S HOW IT WILL WORK FOR YOU TO LOSE WEIGHT, TOO:
Don't discuss it with yourself!

As soon as you've made the decision to do the Challenge, it's time to put blinders on and stop doubting your goals. Stop finding reasons why you can't do the Challenge or why you don't want to. You must want to change something in your life; otherwise, you wouldn't have this book in your hands. All other thoughts are just counterproductive.

The art of losing weight is really about ending the mental debate you have with yourself right from the beginning—starting on the first day of the Challenge. By doing this, every tempting thought that you might have about laziness or stuffing yourself will vanish into thin air in just a few minutes. It's best to ask yourself very briefly if it's worth sacrificing such a wonderful goal just so that you can stuff yourself on one occasion. The pleasure you feel during such a "feeding frenzy" lasts only very briefly, but the frustration you'll feel about the defeat will last for a long time. It's exactly in moments like these that you can easily achieve victories over yourself by simply thinking "No" for just a moment and then finding a distraction.

Success in such long-term projects depends on whether or not you quit questioning decisions that you have made. One thing will help you. With each passing day, it will get easier—the resistance you have to keeping your own rules will get weaker each day. At the same time, your self-confidence will grow and you will believe that you are again able to keep binding agreements with yourself and that you are strong enough to keep them. No matter how many failed attempts you have behind you: this is the way to achieve success.

There's something else that you need to make clear to yourself. If you were successful with the Challenge even one single day, then it won't get any harder, only easier. Tomorrow is also just one day. And it'll definitely be much easier than today. So, focus only on today and not on the time that is still ahead of you—just like a climber should never look down. Eventually, the 30 days will be over and you will have really changed and achieved something.

When I was almost thin, but not quite in shape, this is the way I managed to get a washboard stomach in just 90 days—which is considered to be almost impossible. And it was so nice to have an eight-pack so soon instead of just a six-pack. If you're going to do something, then really do it.

It's important for you to decide what you want and to look ahead—a lot of strength comes from that. Deliberately make up your mind and then: Rock on!

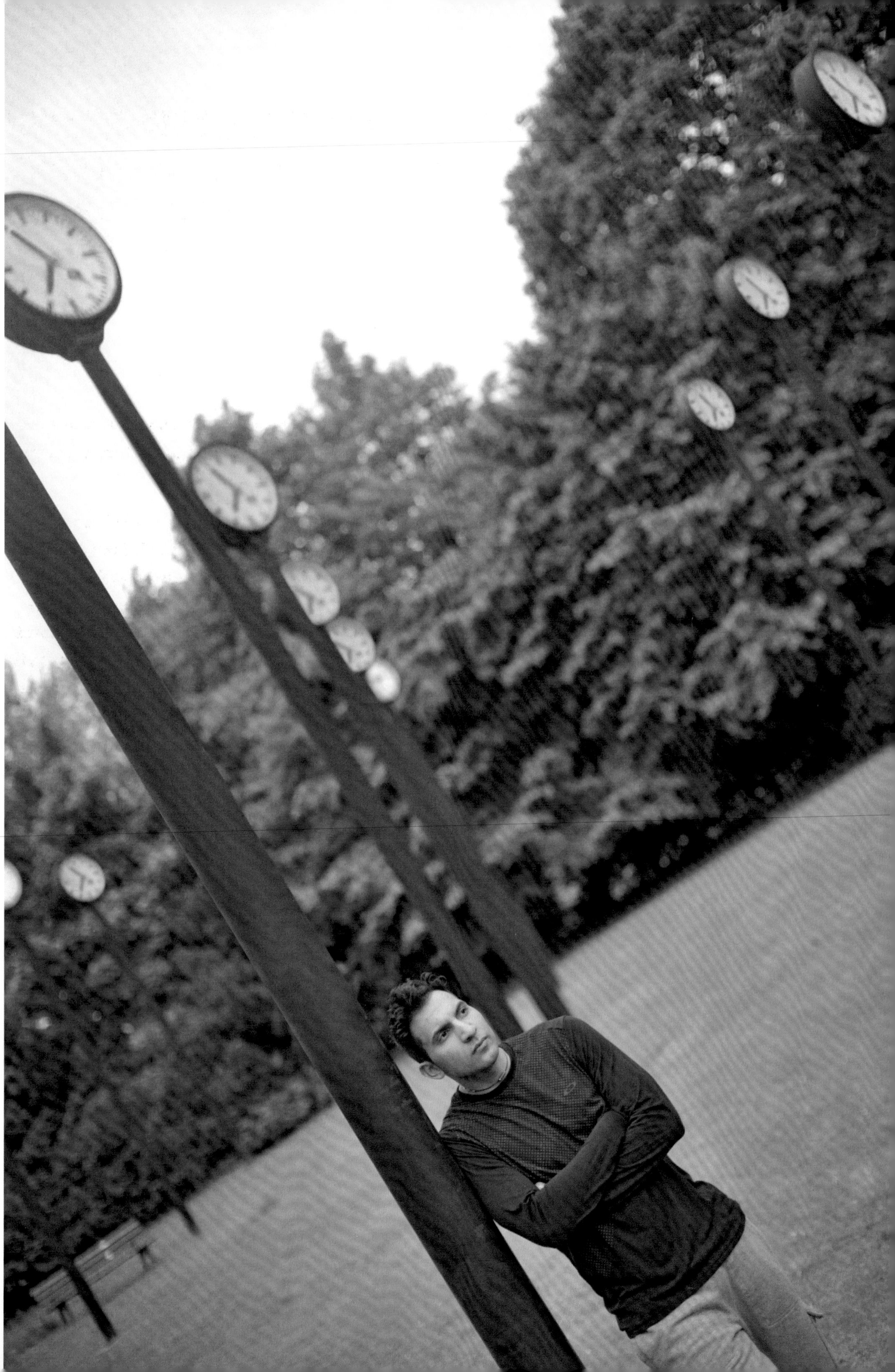

DON'T WASTE YOUR LIFE!
Time is precious. Learn to think actively instead of passively.

I believe that material things are highly overvalued in our world today. Ultimately, you can't take them with you when it's your time to go. But, of course, we don't like to think about our own mortality.

I ask you: how many days do you think that a person lives on average? We would like to think that there are probably half a million or more days. In fact, it's only an average of 28,000 days and that's living to be 76 years old. That's short. Especially, if you consider that you spend about half of your life either at work or asleep. All the more reason why I believe that we should appreciate every day that we have on this planet. It helps to live every day as if it were the last. When I think about this fact, then I can put my everyday concerns back into the proper perspective. Of course, it doesn't always work, but I try to remember how short life is as often as possible. We often get upset about things that aren't worth it, and forget the things that deserve more attention, such as health, friends, and family.

We shouldn't forget that we don't have so much time left to achieve the goals that are important to us. So then, it makes sense to get your body back into shape in 30 days, and then to have a better foundation for the remaining of the 28,000 days. Let's take 30 days to rock and to achieve what we want. After that, we can move on or start looking for the next challenge.

Look closely at a period of 30 minutes. What are some of the things that we can do in this amount of time? We can watch a sitcom with lots of commercial breaks on TV so that we feel that we have been entertained. Or we can go for a 3 mile run, swim 40 laps at the pool, or bike over to see a good friend and drink a cup of green tea together. And when you have made this decision 30 times in a month, you will have changed your life significantly.

To be a Challenger means to be active in your life again and to avoid times of being passive. Blow the dust off of your dreams, and with joy and strength, start to work on making them a reality. Believe me: do this, and you can only come out a winner!

MORE THAN A DIET

My own well-being, fitness level, and feeling of living in a healthy body are things that I strive for. Along with that, though, comes the really good feeling that you are doing something that goes beyond your own narcissism and that you are helping to make the world a better place. This is not about trying to be a better person than others. But you can hold on to the fact that a vegan diet represents the optimal solution for many problems in the world. As a Challenger, you are taking a stance against factory farming, deforestation, climate change, poverty in the third world, and the waste of resources. One of the main causes of climate change is the methane gas that cows produce. You could say that the polar ice caps are melting because of our hunger for more and more steaks.

It also affects me deeply that a seventh of the world population suffers from hunger—currently, more than a billion people. These people could be fed if we didn't have to use so much of our food to feed stock animals, and if more people would choose to eat an organic vegan diet. I think we have enough time to fight for this.

And isn't it an awesome feeling to protect animal lives for 30 days? Like I said, I'm not a fan of thinking in terms of all or nothing and don't want to tell other people what they should think. For me, every meal and every step we take counts, no matter how small they are. So, you can begin with a vegan diet for 30 days and watch yourself to see if this diet is so good for you that you want to repeat it—perhaps once a week or one week per month or whatever. And if a whole lot of people choose to do this for themselves and to maintain their newfound health, that can bring about more change than any angry, militant dogmatist ever could.

It regularly happens to people that they encounter an almost hostile response from others in their circle, when they start eating vegan. This is probably because meat eaters feel somehow attacked when someone refuses to eat the meat or the "complicity" being offered. For this reason alone, it's a unique experience, to switch sides and see how it feels to live without this kind of complex, one that is brewing in the subconscious of many meat eaters.

Incidentally, many car drivers have the same kind of expansion of their consciousness when they try biking for a change.

POOR ANIMALS,
poor people

I think many of us consume animal products and don't even realize the associated consequences. So, please forgive me for the next few lines and don't misunderstand them as some kind of missionary zeal. I just want to shed some light on certain connections, on the way things really are. Schnitzel doesn't grow in the Styrofoam trays that you see in the refrigerated section of the supermarket. And only those who know about how animal products are actually produced can draw the proper conclusions for themselves. Those who don't want to know should probably just skip this chapter.

Years ago, I decided to research the facts because I was interested in the truth. From this truth, I drew the strength to totally change my diet. I have eaten vegan for eleven years now—up to now, the best decision in my life.

Here are some of the sad circumstances that we ourselves can influence to a certain extent if we would make more of a conscious decision about what we eat.

MEAT AND FISH

Huge areas of rainforest are cut down every year so that the land can be used to raise food for animals. An entire ecosystem is being destroyed, animals are dying out—and someday, we too will feel the consequences because the rainforest produces a large part of the oxygen in the atmosphere.

Many animals are never let out of their cages, and never see the sun. Many abuses occur for no good reason when they are transported; often the bolts that are intended to destroy an animal's brain miss and the throat of the animal is cut while it is fully conscious.

Red meat is suspected to promote colon cancer, is full of saturated fat and cholesterol, and it contains neither fiber nor the vital substances found in plants.

It takes 25,000 liters of water and an enormous amount of animal feed to produce one steak.

Shortly after birth, piglets are castrated without anesthesia and their incisors are cut off, which is a very painful procedure, as you can certainly imagine. Pigs are among the most intelligent animals on the planet.

Whole regions of our earth's oceans have been fished out and the large fishing boats continue to destroy entire parts of the ocean floor with their trawl nets. Often other creatures are caught as well, such as dolphins and sea turtles, the latter being an endangered species. A consequence of this is, for example, the explosion of the jellyfish population. There are no longer enough turtles to keep the numbers of these sea creatures down in a natural way.

As a result of marine pollution, fish often contain a high concentration of heavy metals such as mercury. Mercury accumulates in our body and is suspected to cause cardiovascular disease and nerve damage, promote Alzheimer's disease, and weaken the immune system.

Shrimp farming in countries such as Thailand has devastated entire stretches of land. The shrimp are raised in the shortest time possible and given a lot of chemical substances—including antibiotics—that accumulate not only in the flesh, but also contaminate the soil and the ground water.

Fish feel pain like all vertebrates, are actually very sensitive animals, and they are often slit open without stunning. And that's all done so that we can have tuna fish pizza. Sharks are caught for shark fin soup, their fins are cut off, and then they are tossed back into the sea while still alive, where they die in agony.

Meat consumption contributes to world hunger as vast quantities of feed are needed for the production of meat. One billion people are currently suffering from hunger, and every three seconds, a person dies of malnutrition. In the areas where feed is grown, we could grow a variety of organic products and superfoods, which could protect us from aging, keep us firm, and feed many more people.

EGGS

Male chicks are shredded after hatching or simply killed with poison gas because they can't lay eggs. Each year in the U.S., more than 200 million male chicks are killed in this manner. If we were to do the same thing to cat or dog babies, no one would be able to bear the idea.

Eggs contain a lot of cholesterol in the egg yolk, but no vital substances or fiber, and are—from the scientific perspective—actually unborn chicks. For me personally, this isn't an appetizing thought.

MILK

Dairy cows are impregnated every year because only a pregnant cow can provide a high milk yield over many years. It sounds like a perverted porn movie: the so-called inseminator approaches the cow from behind and uses his whole arm and a dose of bull sperm to impregnate the cow. The cow's children, the calves, are a surplus product and are sold cheaply to make Wiener Schnitzel. They are kept for three months in a fattening phase, are often fed only powdered formula, and are separated from their cow mothers. In many cases, the intensively bred mother cows suffer from a painful inflammation of the udder. And sooner or later, milk cows end up in a burger restaurant.

No animal in the natural realm drinks the milk of another species—we humans do so because of how we were brought up and what we see in advertising. Dairy products caused me to get acne, and I often had a slimy feeling in my mouth. In addition, milk aggravated my eczema and milk products in general raised my cholesterol to a critical level. There are many people who are lactose intolerant. Lactose is the name of a sugar found in cow's milk. If the body can't form lactase—that's the name of the enzyme that splits lactose—indigestion is the result.

Throughout the course of history, we have needed and used animals and in hard times, we have drunk their milk. Today, we have ingenious alternatives: plant-based milks are, in my opinion, not only healthier, but just sexy!

Dairy products such as cheese and cream are calorie bombs and rich in unhealthy fat. Cheese was discovered by accident a few centuries ago when fermented milk that had curdled was found in a calf stomach. In Asia, there isn't a cheese culture as there is in Europe and the U.S.—there people are likely to choose more soy products such as tofu. Many Asians can't handle milk and are lactose intolerant.

Throughout history, people have eaten meat and animal products for a long time; however, the conditions in the livestock industry today are more shameful than ever before—which is no wonder, since our planet is now home to seven billion people. The conventional food industry has become a gigantic mass market that a few people without scruples are using for personal gain. But at the checkout stand, you can give your vote as to whether or not this greed and unscrupulousness will have a future. Organic foods and alternative vegetarian products are a huge step in the right direction.

One more thing I think about is that the human race would not yet be so far in the field of advanced technology if we had not exploited animals for thousands of years for our needs. It started with the oxen that pulled plows through the field. It continued with animals being used for medical research and animals whose sole purpose it seems is to serve as inexpensive food.

I just wish that we would recognize the progress we have made thanks to animals. We wouldn't have gone to the moon and wouldn't have the internet or modern quantum physics, without the work of the animals over the previous centuries. Simply said, if we don't have to plow the field and can make the oxen do it, then we have enough time for art, culture, and science. Our civilization and modern medicine is virtually based on the sweat and pain of animals. Perhaps it is time for us to give something back to them or at least not eat them for dinner, when today there are so many delicious and healthy alternatives out there. Let's just say thank you for a change and eat a delicious vegan dish, maybe once a week or once a day or maybe more often.

YOUR LIFE IS A GAME—
Just press "PLAY"!

We live in a society that teaches us to be passive media people. After school or work, we flip through the TV channels, surf the internet, or play video games.

It's only been a few years ago that my TV was always on, day after day in the background. The constant input made me nervous, most programs only entertained me a little, and the news reports on areas in crisis and the evening news made me worry. All this weakened my psyche—I was a fat young man trapped in his fears and somehow controlled by advertising stimuli.

I wasted many nights on my PC online strategy games, rather than making sure I had everything taken care of for my university classes. I was addicted to playing and fighting together with others, and especially to winning! I neglected my family, my girlfriend, and my friends and buried myself further into my fantasy world. I began to dream about the computer games—my account balance and my psyche began to suffer. There came a day when I asked myself a question that would change my life: "If you die one day and look back on your life, do you want to see that you wasted it in a virtual reality? "

Computer games and television programs are really just a waste of time. They are just images of a false reality. A computer game programmer could never ever reconstruct the complexity of reality. No television series in the world could ever reflect a tangible reality. There is no great high score that has any real value to help you solve even one single problem.

I thought about this for several days. Did I really want to spend my life in the artificial reality of a programmer or TV writer? Should this person be the creator of my world and make the rules for me, so to speak, be my God? The idea became more and more repulsive to me and then I did what was previously unthinkable: I uninstalled all my games, threw my TV out of the house, and decided to no longer just be passive.

Ever since that day, I have only watched movies and documentaries on the internet or DVD, and then, only the ones I really wanted to see. This saved a lot of time and there weren't any commercial blocks where every fifteen minutes, I was being presented with irresistible goodies.

Instead, I began to cook a lot more for myself because I realized that it made me happy to use pure, fresh ingredients to conjure up something delicious in just minutes. The next thing I did was to totally clean up my life. I set goals for myself, began to implement them, and started to lay the foundation for financial freedom, by finding a job at the university. It was like I was crazy, instead of going to one class a day, I was going to seven.

It felt good. I was changing something in my life, I had more time again for my mother, my friends, and my girlfriend, and my depressive lethargy disappeared all by itself. I was swimming instead of hanging out in virtual space, and early in the morning I rode my bike to the university or to go work out: that made me happy.

As an ex-computer game junkie, I realized one thing that would affect my whole future. Just like when I was playing the game to collect minerals and gas to build my units and send them off to war, I was now suddenly, in real life, the character who needed to be built up. Education, physical fitness, inner strength, and financial freedom were the new mission objectives for my own game character.

Once we understand reality as the most important game of all, it's adrenaline-charged and more exciting than any computer game. Our possibilities are almost limitless, when we engage with life just like we do in a game: with joy, courage, imagination, and confidence.

In reality, though, we only have one life. It is precious—and that's the reason why we shouldn't waste it. Let's live our dreams and begin to be active! The questions that we need to ask ourselves on a daily basis are ones like these: should we watch a TV show or should we spend two hours with our family? Should we watch the same news three times a day and load ourselves down with the repetition of negative headlines—or go for a run through the park? Should we surf the chat rooms and portals endlessly, check our email ten times an hour—or should we go to a club or a café and get to know real people in the real world?

Every day, we have the choice. Let's make every day we have the best day of our lives, and then every day, we will get just a little bit closer to our goals!

CONGRATULATIONS!

SUCCESS STORIES

SHARED PAIN IS HALF THE PAIN:
It's easier in a group.

Congratulations, you're now a Challenger! Whether you prefer to do the plan alone or if you believe that a group would help you to achieve your goals depends on what type of person you are. But there's one thing you should think about.

There are many people who believe that they do best or prefer to be on their own who would be much more successful in a group. But for many people, joining a group is, for a variety of reasons, a great effort. But here, too, why not just try it?

The first Challenger group, which included people with the most different personalities and life stories imaginable, developed an overwhelming sense of community after just a few days. It was based on respect, tolerance, and cohesion. This thrilled and touched me and the others.

No one has to or had to pay any money or fulfill any obligations in order to participate in the Challenge group. I was simply interested in putting together a great and strong team of 100 men and women who could see if the system that had been tested on a small number of people could successfully be put into practice and if it had any weaknesses.

I didn't have any expectations before meeting the participants—and do you know what happened? At the first Challenger meeting, I was given some hand-painted pictures and a starting place in the "2013 Challenge Roth" held near Nuremberg. You can't imagine how surprised and delighted I was. Doing a long distance triathlon is something I've dreamed of for years.

This spirit of giving without expecting anything has remained a part of this group. We've exchanged our little secrets, laughed together, suffered sore muscles together, and motivated each other with daily photo and video updates. It reminded me of when I was a young boy at summer camp—just now, I'm much more aware. And the group continues!

Melanie

Xandra

Sabine

Chahid

Sandra

Dirk

If you want to be a part of this team spirit write to me on Facebook and join the official group at www.facebook.com/groups/vegansforfitworldwide because together we are stronger and better able to persevere. When other group members comment on what you've achieved, it will totally motivate you. All posts can, of course, only be viewed by other Challengers, and this makes sense since sometimes people post their before and after photos or share their deep frustrations. I look forward to the next Challenger meeting, and perhaps you will be there, too. You don't have to paint a picture—I promise!

PRINCIPLES OF THE CHALLENGER GROUP

I am firmly convinced that together we can improve many things in this world—little by little—if we first change ourselves, before beginning to think about changing other people. Here it's not about whether you will eat meat for the rest of your life or not. If you start eating meat again after the Challenge, that's up to you. It should instead be about the shared goals that connect us during this time. Challengers should understand this spirit and adhere to the following principles during the time together:

- Be loyal to other Challengers.
- Show team spirit and be there for weaker people.
- Be honest with yourself and others.
- Treat each other with respect; avoid controversy.
- Motivate each other.
- For 30 days, remain confident in the face of all those who think they know better in this world.
- Never give up.
- Don't use any animal or industrial products.

Everyone who can imagine doing this for 30 days or longer is welcome to join!

EVERY SINGLE PERSON COUNTS!

Often enough, we give the responsibility for our lives over to others: to our parents and teachers, to professors, finance managers, and politicians. Our earth—when we look at it objectively—is in a state of catastrophe: deforestation, climate change, and melting polar ice caps, an explosive population growth, politicians who do nothing or very little, water and resource scarcity, cosmetics and pharmaceutical industries that torment animals, a seventh of the world's population has nothing to eat, the mountains of garbage are growing, animal species are dying out, child labor is rampant, and dietary diseases are among the leading cause of death in rich countries. We can say, with complete justification, that we—excuse my language—are screwed!

It's actually very easy to change this system, if we realize what power we possess: the power of consumerism. It took me a long time to realize that. But today, I am more convinced than ever that with every purchase we make, we can make the world a little worse or a little better. I've decided for myself that money isn't the most important thing and work together only with companies and manufacturers whose products and means of production I can completely support. I work with companies who have clear organic standards and are involved only in fair trade and fair working conditions for the farmers who grow and produce the products we use. Fortunately, there are several of these.

On the other hand, we have giant corporations that want to privatize water—and that's in a world where drinking water is scarce anyway—and manufacture products to make more profit even though as a result, more people will go hungry or grow sick from malnutrition and an increasing number of animals will have to suffer in factory farms. But it's also true that these companies have only become successful because we are giving them our money. We must make ourselves aware of the role that we play in this situation.

You can't assume that a frozen chicken that sells for $3.99 (2.99 euros) lived a decent life. You can't assume that the conventionally grown bananas have provided money to feed a worker and his or her family and that the worker had a healthy, pesticide-free working environment.

Let's really think about it and simply give our money to those few good companies out there, and support fair projects, sustainable organic agriculture, and companies that make the world a little bit better. I firmly believe that this is possible! And as with anything, it's true that each person counts. However, as I see it, you shouldn't judge people who haven't yet made this connection. Under stress, we all make purchases that aren't thought through. But I believe that it's the will to change, which is the most important, and which will prevail in the long term.

The big question that we have to ask ourselves is: How do we want to experience our world and how do we want to leave it behind? Clean, diverse, and livable—or gray, destroyed, and cruel? Be honest. We actually all know what we need to do! And if everyone does a little, the state of our world will be a lot better tomorrow. It's of no use if one person is doing everything 150 percent correctly, but everyone else does nothing. I believe in the principle that numbers matter and am firmly convinced that if a lot of people make a small change, it really can make a difference. So, let's not wait any longer! Let's do it, let's go out and change the world by using our money to let our voice be heard. Let's stop giving our money to those who only care about making a profit!

Super Easy Baguette with Smoked Tofu, Carrot and Pesto
Level 2

Matcha Shakes
Level 1

Stuffed Tomatoes with Yogurt Nut Cream
Level 1

Chili with Avocado Yogurt Topping
Level 2

You'll find 56 additional great vegan recipes in Attila Hildmann's best-selling cookbook *Vegan for Fun*. You can find recipes that are suitable for the Challenge and the classification of these recipes into Levels 1 and 2 on our www.bjvvlinks.de/1006 under the heading "Vegan for Fun Update."

THE CHALLENGE ON THE WEB
Community and organic suppliers online

Being part of a team and sharing your experience with other Challengers will give you the unique feeling of starting anew. On the internet, you'll find additional information as well as photos of prepared recipes and success stories. You can also post videos and questions and discuss a variety of topics with other Challengers. Be a part of this unique solidarity! In the following list, you'll find links to organic online stores, where you can get the key ingredients for the recipes, and information about vegan bodybuilding and my projects.

www.aiya-america.com
The supplier for organic matcha! Aiya is Japan's largest matcha producer. The growing region is located far from Fukushima. Remember a day without matcha is a wasted day!

www.wholefoodsmarket.com
Eating foods that contain pesticides isn't a good idea. At Whole Foods, you'll find a huge selection of organic products such as amaranth, tofu, nut butters, and vegan snacks for when you're on the go.

www.rapunzel.de/uk
Rapunzel is the organic supplier online for everyone who is looking for a place to buy nut butters and other essential staples at the best prices possible.

www.facebook.com/groups/vegansforfitworldwide
Connect with other Challengers on Facebook.

www.facebook.com/attilahildmannpage
My Facebook fan page is the only place to find up-to-date news and information about me.

www.veganbodybuilding.com
This website is a great way to get your ass in gear and exchange ideas with other athletes who have been vegan for a long time.

INDEX

259

Almond Pea Soup with Walnut Mint Pesto **150**

Amaranth Yogurt Pop with Raspberries and Toasted Coconut Flakes **55**

Amaranth Bars with Cherries and Almonds **169**

Apple Cinnamon Millet Cream **72**

Apple Orange Ginger Shake **201**

Artichoke Cashew Spread **63**

Asian Sesame Burger **157**

Asparagus Orange Soup **161**

Avocado Basil Cream **128**

Avocado Paprika Eggplant Rolls with Sun-Dried Tomato Sauce **111**

Banana Cinnamon Ice Cream **192**

Basil Lime Pesto **128**

Berlin Toast with Cashew Banana Filling and Crunchy Outer Layer **76**

Berry Muesli **57**

Best Snack Bars in the World **169**

Bolognese Spaghetti with Zucchini Noodles and Almond Parmesan Topping **97**

Breakfast Crunch with Almond Milk **71**

Broccoholic—Broccoli with Lemon Almond Cream **119**

Caprese Vegan Style **84**

Carbonara Spaghetti with Zucchini Noodles **94**

Cashew Chocolate Chip Ice Cream **191**

Cashew Panna Cotta with Strawberry Sauce **176**

Cauliflower Curry Crunch **83**

Challenger Fruit Bread **75**

Challenger Breakfast **58**

Chili Crackers **166**

Chocolate Peanut Butter Ice Cream **192**

Cinnamon Bliss Kiss **183**

Coconut Almond Cooler **183**

Coconut Chocolate Bars **196**

Cranberry Coconut Pineapple Muesli **57**

Curry Almond Amaranth with Asparagus in Orange Sauce **86**

Deluxe Walnut Energizer with "I love Salad" Dressing **125**

Eggplant Boats Mexican Style with Thyme Almond Cream **89**

Fast Life Sandwich **67**

Firestarter **64**

Green Tea Cherry Pop **205**

Green Tea Coconut Flow **206**

Green Tea Cream **206**

Green Tea Ginger Minger **205**

Green Tea OJ **207**

Green Tea Pomegranate **207**

Green Warrior **145**

Hazel Chocolate Pralines **183**

Working on this book was a very fruitful journey for me, on which I achieved a lot of personal growth. I would like to thank all of my **CHALLENGERS** for the time we spent together, for the solidarity, and for your feedback. We are a large family and are growing in size daily. I would like to thank **RALF,** the best publisher in the world, for his suggestions, inspiring words, and for the time he took for me. It means a lot to me to have you as a friend! I would also like to thank all of the very hard-working **EMPLOYEES** at the publishing company, who worked tirelessly, professionally, and in a very engaged manner so that this book would be a success. Thank you to **JOHANNA** for contributing to the artistic concept, to **JUSTYNA** for her creative layouts, which everyone loves. Thank you to **ANNE, KATERINA,** and everyone at **BJVV.** The days I spent with you, **SANDRA,** working with you on the photos were one of the highlights of my year. That was pure action, and the photos are world class— and thanks to you, I am now familiar with those amazing Japanese rice balls, Onigiri. **JOHANNES** and **SIMON,** I would like to thank you both for the productive days in the food photo studio, for a fun time and for your dedication to getting the best pictures possible—you've developed a style that has set new standards. I would also like to thank everyone at **KICK MANAGEMENT** for your support and the belief you had in me, even though I'm not always a simple kind of guy. Thank you, **DIANA,** each day that I work with you is more fun. Thank you, **JÜRGEN,** you are and will always be the kind of guy who has a solution for everything. Thank you to **GOETZ, RONJA,** and all the others because without you, we wouldn't be such a strong team. Thank you to **STEPHANIE** and **DOREEN** for your great editing. This time it was quick and painless. Thank you, **HEIKA, GILA,** and **JOSEPH**—I admire your dedication to making this world a better place. Thank you **"CRAZYNOMIS," "THE SPANIARD," TORBEN, DON INDI,** and **AHMED** for your long friendship. You're the coolest and the best! I am very happy, **MOM,** that you are now also a Challenger and that you feel better and healthier—I will always be there for you! Thank you, **DIMI,** for giving me strength, no matter where you happen to be! Thank you, **DEAR BROTHER,** for being there and for helping Mom when I'm sometimes not able to find the time. I am so happy that I was able to spend a chapter of my life with you; I keep you all in my heart! For me, the Challenge has been going on for more than 30 days because life is the biggest Challenge—for all of us. Let's make the best out of it and leave the world behind a better place than we found it! Challengers for life!

PUBLICATION DETAILS

First published by Becker Joest Volk
Publishing Company
© 2013—all rights reserved
First edition: October 2013
ISBN 978-3-95453-012-0

RECIPES AND TEXT Attila Hildmann

FOOD PHOTOS Simon Vollmeyer

FOOD STYLING Johannes Schalk

PORTRAIT PHOTOS Sandra Czerny

PROJECT MANAGER Johanna Hänichen

LAYOUT, TYPOGRAPHICAL DESIGN Anne Krause, artistic concept by Justyna Krzyzanowska for the publicity agency Makro Chroma Joest & Volk OHG

EDITING (GERMAN) Doreen Köstler

EDITING OF RECIPES (GERMAN) Dr. Stephanie Kloster

TRANSLATION Kerstin Gackle

EDITING (ENGLISH) Jason Gackle

PRINTED BY APPL Group, aprinta druck GmbH, Wemding, Germany

**BECKER
JOEST
VOLK
VERLAG**

www.bjv-books.com

Vegan for Fit is also available as an e-book on iTunes or a Kindle version on Amazon.